THE SENSITIVE PLANT

Margaret, Countess of Mount Cashell
From a miniature attributed to Charles Robertson

THE
SENSITIVE
PLANT

A Life of Lady Mount Cashell

By EDWARD C. McALEER

Chapel Hill

THE UNIVERSITY OF NORTH CAROLINA PRESS

To

ARTHUR KYLE DAVIS, JR.

AUTHOR'S NOTE

I FIRST BECAME interested in Lady Mount Cashell when I was a Fulbright Fellow at the University of Rome and Mrs. Flavia Farina-Cini introduced me to the Cini papers. These seemed to be of such human and literary interest that I undertook to make a scholarly study of Lady Mount Cashell. After I had done much research, aided by a grant from the American Council of Learned Societies, I learned that an American scholar had "completed the first draft" of a study of Lady Mount Cashell and her friends in Pisa. Rather than abandon my project, I decided to attempt a somewhat informal volume, addressed to the general reader, including in it all the available material about Lady Mount Cashell as well as background material of the Ireland and Italy that shaped her personality. Such a book required the retelling of much that was already known to scholars in their fields of specialization, but I have tried to retell succinctly, sometimes using the words of the original sources in a reduced scale.

Some critics, following a note by H. Buxton Forman, are not convinced that Lady Mount Cashell was the inspiration of Shelley's "Sensitive Plant." I am. Thomas Medwin tells us that Shelley himself said she was; Shelley wrote the poem in the spring of 1820, precisely when he was most enthusiastic about her in his letters; Mary Shelley went to some trouble to send a sensitive plant to Casa Silva after her husband's death. Shelley identified himself with the plant of his poem, even though he was capable of the most courageous action against cant or injustice. Lady Mount Cashell had the courage to defy society when she left her husband, but for half her life, under an assumed name, she displayed an almost fanatic sensitivity in her desire to protect herself and her daughters from English visitors. When Thomas Jefferson Hogg was received at the Villa Archinto, he wrote to Jane Williams that he was "the first stranger, who ever broke the spell." I have given this book its title because Lady Mount Cashell was a sensitive woman and the inspiration of Shelley's poem, but I do not mean to imply that she was the plant of the poem. Shelley was that; she was the lady who tended the garden.

It is pleasant to have this opportunity to thank the friends and scholars who have assisted me: Professor C. L. Cline, Mr. Oliver D. Gogarty, Professor Leslie A. Marchand, Miss Eleanor L. Nicholes, Professor Lewis Patton, Professor Oreste Rinetti, the late Mr. Thomas U. Sadleir, Dr. Redcliffe N. Salaman, F.R.S., Mrs. M. J. Stocking, Mrs. Giuliana Artom Treves, and Professor Ralph M. Wardle. Members of the Kingston family to whom I am obliged are Lady Brigid King-Tenison, Captain Robert D. King-Harmon, R.N., and Sir Cecil Stafford-King-Harmon. I am grateful for the kind help given me by Lady Mount Cashell's descendants in Italy and Ireland: the Marchesa Trigona, Mr. Neri Farina-Cini, and Captain Rowland Holroyd-Smyth.

Especial thanks are due to those who allowed me to use unpublished material: to Lord Abinger, who has made his Shelley collection available to scholars; to the Keeper of Manuscripts of the British Museum, who allowed me to consult material in the Ashley Library; to Sir John Murray, who allowed me to use material in his Byron collection; to Captain King-Harman; and to Mr. Farina-Cini. Above all, I wish to thank Mrs. Flavia Farina-Cini for her kindness, helpfulness, and hospitality.

The Richmond Area University Center and the Research Committee of the University of Virginia have made grants to assist me in the expenses of travel and manuscript preparation, for which I am most grateful.

The following have granted permission to quote copyrighted material: Ernest Benn, Ltd., and Charles Scribner's Sons to quote from *The Complete Works of Percy Bysshe Shelley;* Messrs. John Murray and Lady Mander to quote from R. Glynn Grylls' *Claire Clairmont;* the University of Oklahoma Press to quote from *The Letters of Mary W. Shelley,* edited by F. L. Jones; the late T. U. Sadleir to quote from *An Irish Peer on the Continent.*

EDWARD C. MCALEER

CONTENTS

CONTENTS

ILLUSTRATIONS

From the Collection of Neri Farina-Cini of San Marcello

THE SENSITIVE PLANT

A Lady, the wonder of her kind,
Whose form was upborne by a lovely mind
Which, dilating, had moulded her mien and motion
Like a sea-flower unfolded beneath the ocean,
Tended the garden from morn to even.

P. B. SHELLEY, *The Sensitive Plant*

INTRODUCTION

ONE DAY late in September of 1819, Percy Shelley interrupted his journey from Leghorn to Florence in order to stop for a day in Pisa to visit a Mrs. Mason who lived there in a modest house on the Via Mala Gonella with her two daughters, Laura and Nerina. He was taking his wife and her step-sister, Claire Clairmont, to Florence, for Mrs. Shelley was approaching confinement and needed the good medical care that Florence could provide.

A few months later Shelley mentioned Mrs. Mason in a letter he wrote from Pisa to Leigh Hunt in England. "We see no one but an Irish lady and her husband, who are settled here," Shelley said. "She is everything that is amiable and wise, and he is very agreeable. You will think it my fate either to find or to imagine some lady of 45, very unprejudiced and philosophical, who has entered deeply into the best and selectest spirit of the age, with enchanting manners, and a disposition rather to like me, in every town that I inhabit. But certainly such this lady is."[1]

Shelley's description of her mind and personality is matched by a description of her appearance which Claire Clairmont wrote years later. "She was very tall," Claire said, "of a lofty and calm presence. Her features were regular and delicate; her large blue eyes singularly well-set; her complexion of a clear pale, but yet full of life, and giving an idea of health. Her countenance beamed mildly, with the expression of a refined, cultivated, and highly cheerful mind. In all my intercourse with her I never saw the slightest symptom of the melancholy and discontent which was so striking both in Byron and Shelley. She was ever all hopefulness and serenity and benevolence; her countenance was 'perfectly irradiated by these sentiments, and at the same time [by sentiments] of purity and unconscious sweetness and beauty."[2]

One curious fact about Mrs. Mason was that her "husband," whom Shelley found "very agreeable," was not called Mr. Mason. Mrs. Mason and the two children called him "Tatty"; his name was, actually, George William Tighe. When Laura was nine and Nerina three, Mrs. Mason, realizing that her two girls would one day be puzzled by this Mason-Tighe discrepancy, sat down and wrote the following document in order that the girls, when they came to be young ladies, would have an explanation:

"In case Laura & Nerina should be left orphans at an early age it appears right that there should be a written document to give them some idea of their Mother's story. It is for this reason I write the following pages.

"Ireland is my native land. My father Robert King Earl of Kingston, was married very young to his relation Caroline FitzGerald. I was the second of their twelve children & being born in that rank of life in which people are too much occupied by frivolous amusements to pay much attention to their offspring I was placed under the care of hirelings from the first moment of my birth—before three years old I was subjected to the discipline of governesses & teachers whose injudicious treatment was very disadvantageous to my temper. As I advanced in years I had various masters (for no expence was spared to make me what is called accomplished) and at a very early age I was enabled to exhibit before my mother's visitors, whose silly praises would probably have injured me if I had not suffered so much in acquiring the means of obtaining them that they afforded me no pleasure. With this sort of education it is not extraordinary that I should have learnt a little of many things & nothing well. Various circumstances having combined to give me a premature disgust to the follies of dress, equipage & the other usual objects of female vanity, mine was early directed towards mental acquirements & at the age of seventeen I felt more flattered by a compliment to my understanding from an old clergyman than by any homage to my beauty from the most fashionable young men of the day. This might have been turned to advantage in more favourable circumstances, but the society of my father's house was not calculated to improve my good qualities or correct my faults; and almost the only person of superior merit with whom I had been intimate in my early days was an enthusiastic female who was my governess from fourteen to fifteen years old, for whom I felt an unbounded admiration because her mind appeared more noble & her understanding more cultivated than any others I had known—from the time she left me my chief objects were to correct those faults she had pointed out & to cultivate my understanding as much as possible: my intentions were good but I wanted advice, perhaps more than those who had less exalted views. I was therefore guilty of numerous errors & none greater than that of marrying at nineteen a man whose character was perfectly opposite to mine. Stephen Moore Earl of Mount Cashell was about one & twenty, a handsome man with gentle manners & the appearance of an easy temper. His education had been of the meannest sort; his understanding was uncultivated & his mind contracted. He had an aversion to literature, was incapable of comprehending the feelings of a noble spirit & respected nothing but wealth & titles—how he came to think of me for a wife God alone knows. To my shame I confess that I married him with the idea of governing him, the silliest project that ever entered a woman's mind. I soon discovered the impossibility of putting this design into execution; for though stewards, housekeepers, grooms &c. found it easy to obtain influence over him, the means by which they acquired this power were such as I could never have deigned to employ. No person was ever worse calculated for such an attempt as I could neither assume the lofty tones of a domineering wife nor the wheedling accents of an humble flatterer. However (after some quarrelling in the beginning) we went on for several years with tolerable tranquillity. I nursed my children, lived chiefly in the country & found my principal amusement in books. At length the political disturbances in Ireland, at the same time that they augmented the number of my errors, gave a firmer tone to my character & thus widened the distance between Lord M. & me. My children also being grown old enough to make their education an object of importance in my eyes, that became a constant subject of dispute, as their father (who loved nothing so well as money) could not endure the idea of going to any expence for a purpose which appeared to him so insignificant. I had been about ten years married when Lord M. was persuaded to make an excursion to the continent & I then ceased to lead the retired life to which I had adapted myself in my own country. The more I saw of society & the farther I travelled the more contemptible Lord M.'s character appeared; however though I often wished to be liberated from his company, I loved my children too well to make any positive effort for a separation, which had been more than once talked of but never seriously discussed. I had not happened to meet with any other man to whom I could have wished myself united & therefore though I felt less regard for him every day yet I had not the most distant apprehension of the errors I have since fallen into. Indeed at thirty I considered myself perfectly secure from either inspiring or being inspired with the passion of love. In the beginning of 1804 a very dull British circle at Rome was rendered interesting to me by the arrival of George William Tighe, a man who would have appeared to advantage in society of a very superiour order: it is not therefore extraordinary that I should have distinguished him from the vulgar crowd or that he should have been attracted by the person most capable of appreciating his merit. A combination of circumstances promoted our intimacy & augmented our admiration of each other; neither of us had sufficient resolution to withstand a strong passion & for years we suffered a variety of anxieties & difficulties. Misfortune must ever be the lot of those who transgress the laws of social life.

"In 1805 Lord M. left me in Germany & from that time I have never seen him. The loss of my seven children was one of the severest punishments of my misconduct, but the reflection that I could never have been of any service to them & the certainty that other people had more influence to obtain for them some degree of education, in a short time reconciled me to this separation: and the birth of Laurette in 1809 consoled me for the privation of the others. The birth of Nerina in 1815 has added to my stock of comfort as I have the satisfaction of knowing that their father will give them the best education possible & will not neglect any thing that may be for their advantage. ——And now that I have competent means of subsistence & that time & misfortunes have corrected many of my faults, I am perfectly satisfied with my lot & hope to pass the remainder of my days with those I love best in the world, in that middle rank of life for which I always sighed when apparently destined to move in a higher sphere.

"Pisa—April—1818

"Laura & Nerina have four brothers & three sisters— their brothers are Stephen Moore Lord Kilworth; the honble. Robert Moore now a Captain in the Guards; the honble. Edward George Moore at the University of Cambridge; & the honble. Richard Francis Stanislas Moore, at present at Westminster school. (Nerina has some resemblance to Robert & Richard)—their sisters are Lady Helena Eleanor, married to Mr. Robinson eldest son of Lord Rokeby; Lady Jane Eliza Moore; & Lady Elizabeth Anne Moore who is about five years older than Laurette—of all these the only one with whom I keep up a correspondence & whom I have seen within these ten years is Robert, who is of so amicable a disposition that I shall venture to leave a letter informing him of the existence of Laura & Nerina in case they should ever have occasion to seek for the protection & affection of a brother. It is scarcely necessary for me to add that Laura & Nerina could never expect to be acknowledged by any of their mother's relations—before they read these lines they will be old enough to understand their own situation in life."[3]

THE HONORABLE MARGARET KING

CHAPTER 1.

THE GALTEES, which form part of the boundary between the County Cork and the County Tipperary, are a range of seven pale-blue, cloud-piercing mountains, named, from east to west, Temple Hill, Knockateriff, Lyracappul, Carrignabinnia, Slievecushnabinnia, Knocknanuss, and Galteemore. The tallest of these is Galteemore, which rises precipitously, almost perpendicularly, to a height of three thousand feet, the third highest mountain in Ireland. The top of Galteemore, shaped like a saddle, has two peaks, between which lies a broad, level terrace a quarter of a mile in length. In the days when there were gods, the Irish gods convened here; and Edmund Spenser, whose Kilcolman Castle (the gift of Queen Elizabeth) lies a few miles to the southwest, chose this belvedere for Dame Nature's court in *The Faerie Queene*. Spenser called the range "Old Father Mole,"

which doth overlooke
The richest champian that may else be rid,
And the faire Shure, in which are thousand salmons bred.

He was describing the view to the north, the Golden Vein of Tipperary watered by the River Suir. Limerick and the River Shannon are to the west, and farther north and east, the Slieve Bloom Mountains.

The south side of Galteemore, cut into bold escarpments by deep gullies in the sandstone, looks down into County Cork on a long plain bounded by mountains and watered by winding rivers. The principal river, the Funcheon or the "ash-growing river," rises in the Galtees, falls into a succession of smooth pools in red sandstone basins, twists its way through innocent valleys and through the demesne at Mitchelstown, and, after a course of thirty miles, flows into the Blackwater. On its way through the plain, it waters what was once the estate of the Earls of Kingston, an estate extending from Kildorrery to Clogheen and occupying one hundred square miles in the Counties Cork and Limerick and Tipperary. Arthur Young, the most distinguished agriculturalist that England has produced, stood on the terrace of Galteemore in the year 1777 and observed that Mitchelstown, in the plain at his feet, had "a situation worthy of the proudest capital."[1]

The mountains are noted for their rivers alive with trout, their waterfalls, and their lakes, said to be unfathomable and of volcanic origin. In one of these, Lough Cuna, St. Patrick, according to tradition, has imprisoned a serpent until some indefinite Monday when the serpent will be freed. Every Monday during the centuries since the time of Patrick, the serpent raises its head above the surface of the water and wearily exclaims, "It is a long Monday, Patrick."[2]

Directly to the east of the mountain range are the Mitchelstown Caves, or New Caves, discovered in 1833, which consist of a mile and a half of limestone caverns, the finest in the British Isles. The caves Arthur Young visited were the old caves, known as the Caves of the Grey Sheep or Skeehewrinky. The walls, ceiling, and floor, composed of every fantastic form, take on the appearance of a vaulted cathedral supported by massive columns.

The spar, formed by the dripping water, glitters brilliantly in pillars, frail drapery, and icicles. These caves have been known to the people since 1601 as Desmond's caves, for it was here that the Sugan Earl of Desmond was hiding when he was captured by the White Knight and sent to the Tower of London.

2

The Earls of Desmond, whom Macaulay called "the greatest and proudest subjects that any Sovereign of Europe ever had," ruled for centuries a great part of Southern Ireland, from Youghal, on the east coast, to Tralee, on the west. Gerald FitzGerald, the fifteenth Earl (and the "Rebel Earl" as well) clashed with Queen Elizabeth for complicated reasons: he was too proud a Geraldine to submit to her intrusion in his territory; furthermore, Elizabeth had a personal preference for another Irishman, the Earl of Ormond, Desmond's enemy, whom she called her "black husband." After years of struggle, Desmond and the Geraldines were defeated, and on one day in 1586 his entire estate of 574,628 acres (probably a million present-day acres) was parceled out to English planters. Edmund Spenser received three thousand.

James FitzThomas FitzGerald, the Sugan (or "straw-rope") Earl, nephew of the defeated rebel, bided his time until 1598 when he broke into rebellion with an army of eight thousand clansmen. Defeated by Elizabeth's Essex, he went into hiding in the woods and in caves, hoping for help from Spain to restore the Desmonds to their old estates. There was a price on his head, but no informer against him could be found among the Irish, for he was "beloved of all sorts," and "such is the superstitious folly of these people," the English officials reported, "as for no price may he be had, holding the same [informing] to be so heinous as no priest will give them absolution." Sir George Carew, assigned the task of capturing him, roamed the countryside, burning houses and corn fields with the aim of forcing the people to inform. The people remained uncorrupted, but a traitor was finally found—a kinsman. Edmund FitzGibbon, the White Knight, motivated by the desire for £1,000 and an estate, captured the Sugan Earl in the Mitchelstown Caves where he was hiding and delivered him in chains for transport to the Tower of London, where he died.[3]

Under a charter of 1259 in the reign of Henry III, John FitzThomas FitzGerald, a cadet of the House of Desmond, gave his three sons the appellations of The White Knight, The Knight of Glin, and The Knight of Kerry. Although not bestowed by a king, the titles were considered hereditary. It was on May 29, 1601, that Edmund, the last White Knight, betrayed the Sugan Earl of Desmond; soon thereafter he received his rewards—the sum down, restoration to his ancient blood and lineage and to the great estate at the foot of the Galtees.

But his betrayal purchased for him the general malice of the people, who took ineffectual refuge in poetry and legend.

> The sternest pulse that leaves the heart to hate
> Will sink o'erlabored, or with time abate.
> But on the clan FitzGibbon, Christ looks down
> For ever with unmitigated frown.
> Did mercy shine—their heart's envenomed shrine,
> Even in her beam, would quicken to new crime.[4]

The legend grew that the old Earl of Desmond's body lies enchanted under the waters of Lough Gur. Every seven years he awakes and rides over the surface of the lake on a horse shod with silver, attended by his knights. When the silver shoes are worn to the hoof, the Earl of Desmond will return to restore his lost glories, Ireland will be free, and the curse will fall from the clan FitzGibbon. People who believe in curses might say that this one soon took effect: the White Knight lived just long enough to see his son and heir die before he died himself in 1608. Ironically, his treachery had preserved land, wealth, and title, but no male heir to inherit; the title died with him.

His lands passed to his kinswoman Margaret Fitz-Gibbon, who, a little girl of eleven, obediently married and endowed with all her worldly goods Sir William Fenton, son of the Secretary of State for Ireland and brother-in-law of the first Earl of Cork. The Earl of Cork wrote in his diary: "December 29, 1614. My brother William Fenton, was married, in my house of Youghal, by Mr. Sneswell, the Preacher, to Margaret Neen Morrish Gibbon, heir-general to the White Knight, which young couple I beseech God to bless and prosper."[5] God's blessing did not include a son and heir; a daughter, Catherine Fenton, representative of the White Knight and heir to his estates, married the second Sir John King, later to become the first Baron Kingston. By this marriage, the Kingstons acquired possession of the lands—and of the curse.

3

The King family, anciently seated at Feathercock Hall near Northallerton in Yorkshire, had come to Ireland in the days of Queen Elizabeth. Sir John, the first-comer, had been sent as a soldier with the assignment of reducing the Irish to due obedience. He was rewarded by Elizabeth with a lease of the Abbey of Boyle in County Roscommon, an abbey founded in 1161 by Maurice O'Duffy and forced into dissolution in 1569. The Kingston family which he founded acquired great estates in Roscommon, Limerick, Cork, and Tipperary, and was three times elevated to the peerage. Sir John died in 1636, a year before his younger son Edward was drowned. Edward King was a fellow at Cambridge University preparing himself for holy orders when the ship on which he was returning to Ireland sank. His friends published a commemorative volume, which is still well known because it contains *Lycidas*, the monody in which John Milton bewails his learned friend, unfortunately drowned in his passage from Chester on the Irish Seas.

The second Sir John King, a grandson of the first, married Catherine Fenton and succeeded in right of his wife to the extensive lordship of Mitchelstown. He was as astute as the Vicar of Bray in backing winners: his zeal in supporting Oliver Cromwell during Cromwell's ravishment of Ireland was surpassed only by his later zeal for the restoration of Charles II. The restored Charles advanced him to the peerage in 1660, creating him first Baron Kingston of Kingston.

Robert, his eldest son, became the second baron, but he died young and the title passed to the next son, John, third Baron Kingston. John, who conformed to the Roman Catholic religion, married Margaret O'Neill O'Cahan, descendant of the O'Cahans of Londonderry and, on her mother's side, of the O'Neills of Clare. Irish blood—FitzGibbon, O'Neill, O'Cahan—thenceforth flowed in Kingston veins. Lord Kingston attended the Catholic James II during that king's Irish campaign—his zeal for James equaled his father's zeal for Cromwell—but James's cause was a lost one, so lost that the third Baron Kingston was deprived of his title and estates on the accession of the Protestant William and Mary. A few years later, William and Mary accepted his oath of allegiance, and the estates returned to the representatives of the White Knight.

His son James, the fourth baron, fortunately of the Protestant persuasion, established Kingston College, an unusual philanthropy which still operates in Mitchelstown. He set aside £25,000 from the Kingston estate to provide homes for twelve decayed gentlemen and twelve decayed ladies, members of the Established Church, each inmate receiving free of rent and taxes a house and garden with an annual pension of forty pounds. A typical little two-story stone house contains four rooms, a great glory hole, a turf house; each garden contains about four hundred square yards, just enough for one decayed gentle person to tend. The houses, unified into one façade with a chapel in the middle, occupy three sides of King's Square. The chaplain, in return for a chaplaincy and an annual income, is required to conduct morning and evening prayers daily, preach a sermon every Sunday, and administer the sacrament at Easter, Whitsuntide, and Christmas. Each member of the college is expected to attend the services and to be in residence at least ten months of the year. Since it is easier to find decayed ladies who wish to attend church twice daily than it is to find similarly inclined decayed gentlemen, the number of ladies was soon increased to eighteen. Today, the original sixteen dwellings have increased to thirty-one, and about forty people are in residence, beneficiaries of the fourth Baron Kingston.[6]

Upon the death of the fourth Baron Kingston in 1761, for the third time in five generations there was no male heir to inherit. The title became extinct and the estate passed to his daughter, Margaret King, who married Richard FitzGerald of Ophaley, a Geraldine. Their son died before he could inherit, and their daughter, Caroline FitzGerald, sole heiress of the estates and representative of the White Knight, married her cousin Robert King of Boyle. These were the parents of Margaret, Lady Mount Cashell, the subject of this book.

4

This marriage of cousins was arranged and convenient. Caroline was much sought after, not only because she was at fourteen a beautiful young lady, but also because she would make her husband one of the wealthiest men in Europe. Robert King, at fifteen, was heir to his father's estate in Roscommon as well as heir to the title of his father, Edward King, who had been created Baron Kingston in 1764, Viscount Kingsborough in 1766, and Earl of Kingston in 1768. The union of these two young people, which reunited the estates and fortunes of the Kingston family, was effected with precautionary haste. Lord Kildare, eldest son of the Duke of Leinster, was one who sought the hand of Caroline, and she might at any moment yield to the temptation of becoming a duchess.[7] The estate at Mitchelstown was held in trust for her until she came of age. After the marriage, on December 5, 1769, at St. Michan's Church in Dublin, Robert, by courtesy Lord Kingsborough, did not return to Eton, but settled with his bride in his father's Dublin house at 15-16 Henrietta Street. His education was continued under the direction of a secretary-tutor, Mr. Tickell.

Young Lady Kingsborough did not get on well with her mother-in-law, Lady Kingston. After a series of quarrels, Lord Kingsborough decided to move his family from Ireland until his wife reached her majority. On December 16, 1772, he left Kingstown in the mail packet, taking with him his wife, his children George and Margaret, a nurse, and Mr. Tickell. (George had been born in Chelsea in 1771,[8] and Margaret Jane in Henrietta

Street on October 24, 1772.)[9] "My dear Lord," he wrote
to his father from Holyhead, "I have the pleasure to tell
you that we all arrived safe and well, thank God, at
Holyhead about Eleven O'Clock, we were all very sick
except Margaret and her Nurse who were quite well."[10]
They remained in London for a year in a house they rented
on Hill Street, and in December of 1773 Lord and Lady
Kingsborough set off on a tour of the Continent, leaving
the children behind in the care of the nurse and the
servants. The fashionable world in which they moved
was engrossed by the beauty of the pair and particularly
by the youth of the parents still in their teens.

All told, the Kingsboroughs had twelve children.[11]
What became of them in future years significantly il-
lustrates how the army, navy, church, and diplomatic
service were staffed by members of the great families:

George, third Earl of Kingston
Robert, General in the Army, first Viscount Lorton of
    Boyle
Thomas, who died young
Henry, Lieutenant General in the Army, Knight Com-
    mander of the Most Honorable Order of the Bath
Richard FitzGerald, Clerk in Holy Orders, Vicar of
    Great Chesterford
John, Secretary of the Embassy to the Elector of Würtem-
    berg
James William, Rear Admiral in the Royal Navy
Margaret Jane, wife of the second Earl of Mount Cashell
Caroline, wife of Major General Edmund Morrison
Mary Elizabeth, wife of George Galbraith Meares, Esq.
Jane Diana, wife first of Herman, Count Wentringerade,
    and secondly of General John Robert Augustus di
    Ricci
Louisa Eleanor, wife of the Baron de Spaen

The Kingsboroughs returned from their tour in the summer of 1775, stayed briefly in the house on Henrietta Street, and moved to Mitchelstown when Lady Kingsborough reached her majority. When they arrived in Mitchelstown, their family seat, they found the town and country in a state of wretchedness. The agent whom they had employed to manage the estate visited it no more than once or twice a year. He employed a clerk, whose office was a summer house in the castle grounds, whither the tenants came to pay their rents in a succession of driblets. The town was a den of vagabonds, thieves, and beggars; the misery and poverty of the people manifested itself in confusion, disorder, and riot. The vast estate, once a forest, had been, like the rest of Ireland, denuded in the course of the years. Ash, oak, holly, birch, willow, hazel, and white thorn trees had been sold for sixpence apiece and had "gone to England." In their place grew furze, broom, fern, rushes, and desolation. Arthur Young observed that on the estate of a hundred thousand acres "you must take a breathing gallop to find a stick large enough to beat a dog."[12]

Middlemen rented to middlemen who rented to middlemen who rented to tenants, so that three or four drones had to be supported by the man who worked the land before any money was put into the hands of the lord who owned it. By law, Catholic tenants could have only short-term leases, so that toward the end of every lease they abused the land that supported them. By custom, an improved farm cost more to rent, so that tenants made no improvements. Money was so scarce that a tenant would walk ten or twelve miles to a fair with a straw band tied to a lamb which he might sell for three shillings and sixpence. Nothing was too trifling to carry: a yard of linen, a fleece of wool, a couple of chickens.

The peasants, often lineal descendants of great Irish families, lived in unimaginable poverty. The typical cabin consisted of one room with walls of mud and straw only six or seven feet high, without window or chimney, with no floor but the ground. For furniture there was a pot for boiling potatoes, sometimes a table, perhaps some stools; generally there was no bed other than straw on the floor. For food they had potatoes and milk; some never knew the taste of meat, others had meat once a year. The families had cows and pigs (there were more pigs than people in Mitchelstown), but these were not for eating; they were for paying rent to the landlord and tithes to the clergyman. The most unfortunate were the *spalpeens*, wanderers, who would fix themselves under a dry bank and, with a few sticks and furze, make themselves a hovel much worse than an English pigstie. "In my rides about Mitchelstown," Arthur Young wrote, "I have passed places in the road one day without any appearance of a habitation, and next morning found a hovel, filled with a man and woman, six or eight children, and a pig."[13] It would be understandable if the Kingsboroughs threw up their hands and rejoined the absentees in London and Bath who were spending more than a million pounds a year of Irish money.

To explain why they remained, it is necessary to define some of the political conditions of Ireland in the latter half of the eighteenth century. George I and George II had been dull and sluggish kings, apathetic towards Ireland and perhaps quite unconscious of Irish problems. When George III came to the throne in 1760, there was a new promise, a new hope in the air that things were going to get better. He gave evidence of intentions to develop rather than exploit the country, almost his first act being to require that his Lord Lieutenant should reside in

Ireland. The presence of the Vice-regal court gave, in Elizabeth Bowen's words, "prestige, lustre and focus"[14] to Dublin society, which moved against a background of roomy, Palladian elegance. Ireland was in fashion.

Before 1782, the torpid Irish Parliament had no function to speak of; affairs of church and state and market were maneuvered by the Tory party in Westminster under a corrupt and abusive system which produced only despair in the hearts of most Irishmen. But now, in the last quarter of the century, it was apparent that Ireland had to be reckoned with. For one thing, George Washington stood up to George III, and military reverses in the American colonies forced a more conciliatory attitude on the English rulers of Ireland. In 1778 the British Parliament made concessions in favor of Irish trade; the Relief Act lightened somewhat the burden on Catholics. Most of the concessions and relaxations can be credited to the Patriot Party in the Irish Parliament, which functioned from 1760 to 1782, headed first by Flood and then by Grattan. The party aimed at winning for Ireland English constitutional liberties and a parliament responsible only to the King. The Volunteers, who might be considered the military wing of the Patriot Party, passed a resolution "that the claim of any other than the King, Lords and Commons of Ireland to make laws to bind this kingdom is unconstitutional, illegal and a grievance."

The embarrassment of military reverses in America had, of course, effect in England. The Tories went out; the Whigs came in; and the Whigs—men like Fox and Burke—were acutely conscious of and sympathetic towards Irish claims. On May 27, 1782, Irish parliamentary independence was formally recognized; "Grattan's Parliament," as it was known, would henceforth make the laws. In a famous speech, Grattan traced the history of Ireland in his century, a history of wrongs and grievances, culminating in the achievement of an independent parliament. "Ireland is now a nation," he said. "In that character I hail her, and bowing in her august presence I say, *Esto perpetua.*"

One result of the new nationalism, the consciousness of a separate Irish nation, manifested itself in an interest on the part of the gentry in Irish antiquities, music, and dancing. The Royal Irish Academy, to which many of the nobility belonged, did much to encourage the new interest. Gentlefolk began discussing things that long had been ignored: cairns, tumuli, cromlechs, round towers. They began making excursions to places associated with the old Irish civilization, to Cashel, to Tara. They collected Irish manuscripts, they revived the old Irish music, and seriously undertook the study of the Irish language. In the nineteenth century, Anglo-Irish parents were known to forbid their children to sing the Irish melodies; in the days of Grattan's Parliament, things Irish were in vogue.

This was the Ireland that Lord Kingsborough returned to in 1775, the same year, it is noteworthy, that the Americans became openly defiant of English rule. Lord Kingsborough was twenty-one when he returned, dedicated to the role of an "improving landlord" and to the development of his estates and of his country. He had assets which could not be despised. His youth and enthusiasm were supported by an estate of a hundred thousand acres with an income reported in 1799 to be £18,000 a year. His tenants, as Arthur Young noted, were cheerful, vivacious, and voluble people, lacking the incivility and sullenness of the English poor. Although they lived entirely on potatoes and milk, they were strong and healthy. Best of all, they had the old Gaelic affection for

the chieftain; no nobleman in Europe could find more
loyalty among his tenants. They had the will to please
and needed only leadership.

Arthur Young visited Mitchelstown in 1777, two years
after the Kingsboroughs returned, and Lord Kingsborough
liberally assisted him in gathering information for his
projected *Tour in Ireland*. He found that the estate
contained every variety of land from fertile plains to
mountain heath, the whole capable of such improvement
that he prophesied it would become one of the first proper-
ties of Europe. "It is not to be expected," Young said,
"that so young a man as Lord Kingsborough, just come
from the various gaiety of Italy, Paris, and London,
should, in so short a space as two years, do much in a
region so wild as Mitchelstown. . . . Men, who from
long possession of landed property, become gradually
convinced of the importance of attending to it, may at last
work some improvements without meriting any considerable portion of praise; but that a young man, warm from
pleasure, should do it, has much superior claim."[15]

5

Lord Kingsborough first marked off thirteen hundred
acres for his demesne (which in England would be called
a park) and girded it round with a ten-foot wall within
which he planted a belt of mixed woodland. On a rocky
hill touched by the Gradoge on its way to join the
Funcheon and commanding a view of the surrounding
country, he built his spacious, graceful mansion. Imported
Italian artisans worked on the mantels, the plaster, the
ceilings, the grand staircase. From Italy and France
came pictures and statues for his house and gardens; from
all over Europe came books for his library. The construction of the castle gave order and dignity to the

neighborhood, provided work for laborers, and gave the tenants something they could respect and love. It was the manifestation of interest in the land.

From England he brought a skilled nurseryman who directed the construction of his gardens, the "largest and best planted in the kingdom." Behind the castle, statue-studded terraces surrounded a square parterre of flowers; before it, a long avenue planted with treble rows of trees led to the demesne gates. In the center were little fish ponds, pond above pond, on the acclivity of a hill. The whole park, stocked with varieties of deer, was thrown into squares and parallelograms, with avenues fenced and planted, twelve acres of nursery, and "above ten thousand perch of hedges." The kitchen gardens, stable yards, and orchards extended almost to the demesne boundary, some distance from the castle. Stone houses with slated roofs and their own farmyards were provided for the steward and other retainers; substantial cabins were built for some fortunate tenants who rented land within the demesne. Entrance was provided by three gateways, each with its own lodge-house. All the land not used for the pleasure of the family was cultivated or used for grazing his lordship's two hundred sheep and forty horses, the whole manned by one hundred laborers—cowboys, drovers, turfmen, thatchers, smiths, weavers, carpenters, and ploughmen, in addition to domestic servants: steward, housekeeper, butler, footmen, coachmen, valets, ladies' maids, nurses, pantry-boys, cooks, housemaids, tutors, and governesses. And this almost self-sufficient kingdom was but one-hundredth part of the Kingsborough estate.[16]

Mitchelstown (a town of 138 acres as opposed to the 1,300 within the demesne) still retains the planned appearance given to it by Lord Kingsborough. Two main parallel streets run north and south: Cork Street, part of the highway from Dublin to Cork, is for shops and markets; George Street is tree-lined and residential. These are cut at right angles by side streets named after Kingsborough boys—James, Robert, and Edward. Of the two spacious squares, one is the market, for Mitchelstown is a market town; the other, King's Square, contains Kingston College, which overlooks a green planted with lime trees and, beyond, the principal entrance to the demesne. Elizabeth Bowen, whose house Bowen's Court is in the neighborhood, writes, "almost all the houses are painted— pink of all shades, buff, lemon, pistachio green, chalk blue. When sun blazes on to the town and the mountain is in full colour, all this dazzles the eye."[17] When Lord Kingsborough built the town, it dazzled the eyes, and pleased the hearts, and gave orderliness to the lives of the townsmen.

Developing the demesne, building the castle, and constructing the town brought much needed work to the tenants and townsmen, but it was, perforce, work that would come to an end. Lord Kingsborough, aware of this and with commendable vision, saw to it that there were more lasting opportunities for work and trade. Early nineteenth-century reports indicate that by that time the town had a cotton factory, brewery, tan yard, bleach green, flour and woolen mills, tobacco and soap factories, and salt works. By 1820 it was the principal establishment in Ireland of the British, Irish, and Colonial Silk Company, which transplanted four hundred thousand mulberry trees and plants in the neighborhood of Mitchelstown. With the provision of opportunities for work, the town forsook its old riot and became as peaceful a town as there was in the kingdom.

6

Lady Kingsborough's diligence and good will matched her husband's. During his lifetime and during the twenty-four years that "the good countess" survived him, she established and endowed a dozen charities for the poor on her estate. The Reverend Horatio Townsend has nothing but praise for her ladyship in his *Statistical Survey of the County of Cork,* 1810. "Everything however has been done by [Mitchelstown's] present possessor, the Dowager Lady Kingston," he wrote, "which the happy wisdom of charity and affluence could suggest, to enlighten the minds of the rising generation, and ameliorate the condition of the people. Her Ladyship's liberal and munificent expenditures are as follows."[18] Then he lists:

An orphan school, where twelve girls were lodged and taught the three R's, domestic science, and the principles of Christianity.

A new, elegant, and expensive church, which owed almost everything to her ladyship's bounty, including a communion service of "silver double gilt." (The spire of the church, which still stands, has collapsed three times over the years. Catholic chapels in Ireland were not permitted spires.)

A physician, who for sixty pounds a year visited the sick poor and provided them with necessary medicines from the apothecary.

A well-stocked village library.

A public shop where groceries were retailed at wholesale prices.

A second shop, which retailed blankets, sheets, and clothing.

A weaving school, where girls were taught to weave linen

with a texture "as close and fine as that of men's manu-
facture."

A bleach green.

A spinning school, at which all the poor girls of the town
were taught to make listing shoes and to spin flax.

A Sunday school, extended also to Wednesdays and Fri-
days, which enrolled two hundred students.

7

In the spring of 1777 the Kingsboroughs were in
London, at which time Lord Kingsborough complained
somewhat bitterly to his good friend Mr. Danby that his
Irish agent provided the estate with very little but neglect.
He was looking for a resident agent who understood agriculture and who could contribute to the improvement of
his property. Mr. Danby recommended the very man
with whom Lord Kingsborough was already acquainted—
Arthur Young. An agreement was soon reached by which
Young would receive an annual salary of five hundred
pounds and a residence rent-free, with a retaining fee of
five hundred additional pounds paid immediately. It is
a question whether Lord Kingsborough fully appreciated
the value of the man he engaged. "Lively, charming,
spirited Mr. Young," then thirty-five, was already the
author of several books and was later to become England's
greatest writer on agriculture, Fellow of the Royal Society,
Secretary of the Board of Agriculture, and member of
various foreign academies.

Young sent his books and effects to Ireland and spent
some time in "a constant round of Dublin dinners," until
his lordship informed him that his residence in Mitchelstown was ready. In September he moved in; his wife
joined him later. At once he busied himself in examining
the farms that came out of lease. He persuaded Lord

Kingsborough to get rid of the whole race of middlemen by renting directly to the tenant as leases expired. Lord Kingsborough's income would remain the same. Almost everybody thought the arrangement excellent, especially the small farmers who were released from bondage to the middlemen. The farmer was required to pay his rent punctually, of course; but his rent was less and consequently easier to pay. Young also put some of his other ideas into practice. Trees were given to the tenantry, and premiums were offered to those who planted most; eighty pounds a year were offered for a variety of agricultural improvements most wanted on the estate. The tenants could not do too much in their efforts to please their landlord and his new agent. They were pleased; Young was pleased; Lord Kingsborough was pleased; everybody was pleased.

That is to say, everybody but one Major James Badham Thornhill. Major Thornhill, a distant cousin of Lady Kingsborough, had, as a middleman, been rack-renting one farm on the estate and had his eye on another. It seemed to him perfectly fair that he should continue doing nothing for his income and that he should increase it by middlemanning additional farms. He had everything to lose otherwise.

"I was placed," Young says, "in an awkward situation. It was impossible for me, consistently with the interest of Lord K., in any measure whatever to promote the success of designs which struck at the very root of all my plans, as the Major had his eye upon several of the most considerable farms. Lady K. had a high opinion of the Major, who was a lively, pleasant, handsome man, and an ignorant open-hearted duellist; she had of course favoured his plans, and I as carefully avoided ever saying anything in favour of them. Thus from the beginning it was not difficult to see an underground plot to frustrate schemes commencing very early, but things in the meantime carried a fair outward appearance. I dined very often at the Castle, and generally played at chess with Lady Kingsborough for an hour or more after dinner, and I learned by report that her Ladyship was highly pleased with me, saying that I was one of the most lively, agreeable fellows. Lord Kingsborough was of a character not so easily ascertained, for at many different periods of his life he seemed to possess qualities very much in contradiction to each other. His manner and carriage were remarkably easy, agreeable, and polite, having the finish of a perfect gentleman; he wanted, however, steadiness and perseverance even in his best designs, and was easily wrought upon by persons of inferior abilities."[19]

Mrs. Thornhill, "an artful designing woman, ever on the watch to injure those who stood in her husband's way, and never forgetting her private interest for a moment," had her eye on more than farms to rent; she wanted her husband to have Young's job. Her design was at least as old as the design the elders used against Susanna: Lord Kingsborough, she whispered to Lady K., was having an affair with Miss Crosby, the governess. Of course they denied it, but what could one expect? Miss Crosby had to go. Young, as estate agent, was directed to draw up an engagement granting her an annuity of fifty pounds, and, of necessity, went much between Miss Crosby and Lord Kingsborough. Mrs. Thornhill then whispered to her ladyship that Young was a go-between serving master and governess, all three in league. At the same time, Major Thornhill (and this must have been his wife's contrivance) convinced Lord K. that Arthur Young was in love with her ladyship. The Thornhills had everybody coming and going. Young went, with an

annuity of seventy-two pounds, having served the estate
for a little over a year. No doubt Major Thornhill got
his farms and agency; certainly the estate lost a most
distinguished agriculturalist. It is shocking to observe
what two liars can do in search of a job.

8

Meanwhile, Lord Kingsborough's energies were directed not only to the development of his estates and
to the government of his country, as governor of Cork
(1789) and member of Parliament (1783-97), but to the
military defense of his country as well. During the
American Revolution, so large a part of the Irish Army
had been sent to fight for England in America that the
country was in an undefended state. In 1778 John Paul
Jones was able, with impunity, to cast anchor off the harbor
of Belfast; French landings constantly threatened. The
alarmed people appealed to the Government for military
protection; they were told, with good reason, that they
would have to supply their own defense. From this need
the Volunteer Movement arose spontaneously and with
the approval of the Government; within a very short time
the corps throughout Ireland mustered some eighty
thousand trained men.

The Volunteers formed a pyramid of the Protestant
population from grooms to dukes. Brilliantly uniformed,
bristling with muskets, fluttering female pulses, they
paraded and drilled in the little towns up and down the
countryside. Often there were Volunteer reviews—gala
events with bands, dinners, fireworks, and thousands of
spectators. But, more important, they assembled in Dublin and lined the streets in calculated display of armed
menace in time of legislation. It was largely owing to

their existence that Grattan was able to obtain his Constitution in 1782.

It would seem that every village in County Cork had its corps of Volunteers. Of the Mitchelstown Light Dragoons we read: "Enrolled 1774. Uniform: scarlet, faced black, silver epaulets, yellow helmets, white buttons. Furniture: goat-skin, edged black. Officers in 1782—Colonel, Viscount Kingsborough; Lieut.-Colonel, Henry Cole Bowen [from nearby Bowen's Court]; Major, James Badham Thornhill [after his triumph over Arthur Young]; Captain, Harmer Spratt; Lieutenant, William Raymond; Cornet, William Alsop; Chaplain, Thomas Bush; Surgeon, David FitzGerald; Secretary, John Ryan."[20] The town of Kilworth, seven miles from Mitchelstown, had its corps of infantry. We read: "Enrolled 1779. Force: 1 company. Uniform: scarlet, faced green, yellow buttons. Officers in 1782—Colonel, Stephen Earl Mountcashel; Lieut.-Col., Arthur Hyde; Major, John Hyde; Captain, Robert Hendley; Lieutenant, John Drew; Ensign, Lord Kilworth [then twelve years old, the future husband of our Lady Mount Cashell]; Adjutant, Richard Whitford; Chaplain, Hon. Robert Moore; Secretary, Richard Whitford."[21]

9

This was the family into which Margaret King was born, and the setting in which she spent the first nineteen years of her life. As a child she could not have questioned her right to rank and privilege; it was her due. One might like to think that as eldest daughter she was her father's favorite, if a noble lord could be said to know his children well enough to have a favorite. The scrappy evidence we have would seem to indicate that Lord Kingsborough saw but little of his daughter: there were too many hirelings between the nursery and the drawing room. Then, too, Margaret was only a year old when her parents left her in the charge of a nurse while they spent two years on the Continent. Arthur Young does not mention the children. Our next source of information is a woman who lived within the family as governess to Margaret and who was at least as famous as the famous Arthur Young.

CHAPTER **2.**

WHEN THE KINGSBOROUGHS were in residence at Mitchelstown, it was not unusual for the castle to house as many as forty people, members of the family and their guests. Actually, there were two families: the Kingsboroughs and the FitzGeralds, the first consisting of Lord and Lady Kingsborough and their twelve children, the second consisting of Mrs. FitzGerald (Lady K.'s stepmother), three marriageable daughters (Maria, Harriet, and Margaret), and a youngest son and favorite, Henry, who was the same age as Margaret, charming and witty, but of violent temper and "uncultivated," for he was well in his teens before his mother could bring herself to send him off to school in England.[1]

Another member of the family, anomalous but important, was Henry Gerard FitzGerald, the illegitimate and only son of Lady Kingsborough's deceased brother, about five years older than Margaret. All the evidence, and later there is to be a great deal of evidence, shows that he was a lovable and handsome boy, afflicted with the FitzGerald violence of temper. Before his voice changed he was a singer in the Chapel Royal, gifted with so fine a voice as to assist His Majesty George III in worship; as a man, he was considered one of the best officers in His

Majesty's service and rose rapidly to the rank of colonel. If Henry Gerard thought about it at all, he would have had cause for bitterness: had he lived, his father would have been heir to the estates of the White Knight; had his father married his mother, Henry himself would have been heir. But a sinister fate forced this legatee of the White Knight's curse to appear in the role of an illegitimate dependent on Lord Kingsborough's generosity, even though that generosity knew no bounds.

Not the least of the problems which confronted the Kingsboroughs was the task of educating their twelve children, aided or obstructed by a series of migratory governesses, tutors, and masters. The boys had tutors (sometimes a "little clergyman") until they were ten, when they were sent off to Eton and thence to Exeter College, Oxford. (There is a portrait of George by Romney in the Provost's Lodge at Eton.) There were, of course, many private schools in England where girls could be educated, but little girls in the eighteenth century (Jane Austen among them) showed a shocking tendency to contract what was called "putrid fever" at boarding school, and most wealthy parents preferred to keep a resident governess whose instruction was supplemented by visiting masters of modern languages, singing, and dancing.

The ordinary governess taught her girls, with the help of instructive little manuals, to read, to write a flowing hand, to spell and punctuate correctly, to do needlework, to be neat in everything. She was expected to ensure the acquirement of accomplishments—ornamental pastimes for tedious exhibition—and she was also expected to be treated as an upper servant. Late in the century thoughtful parents began to prefer a "person of enlarged and philosophic mind" who could be placed in sole charge of the schoolroom, a person with steadiness of purpose, freedom from prejudice, and integrity rather than accomplishments. Always the parents had to run the risk of getting on the one hand a scatterbrain who would impede knowledge and on the other hand a genius who would spend her time in her room writing novels in which she exposed the follies of her employers.

During the summer of 1786 the Kingsboroughs were in England with their children. Their plans were to leave the boys behind them at Eton and to secure an English governess of enlarged and philosophic mind to go to Ireland to supervise the education of their three oldest girls. Lady Kingsborough communicated her desire to the wife of the Reverend John Prior, an undermaster at Eton who directed the education of her boys. Not pleased with earlier governesses, who had been stronger on ornamental pastimes than on the achievements of the mind, she offered a salary of forty pounds a year for the right young woman to take sole charge of the education of her daughters. Mrs. Prior knew of such a young woman, one who had kept a school of her own and had recently completed a book (not yet published) called *Thoughts on the Education of Daughters*. The young woman was a certain Mary Wollstonecraft.

Mary Wollstonecraft, who was to exert a profound and lasting influence on Margaret, was twenty-seven when she accepted the position. The Kingsboroughs could not know that they were engaging a woman who was to achieve in the next decade a celebrity throughout Europe greater perhaps than that of any other woman writer. Mary, whose Irish mother submitted to a drunken and despotic husband, had been subjected to such abuse and continual restraint at home that she freed herself, when nineteen, by taking a position as companion to a wealthy widow at Bath and for two years endured the tyranny and humilia-

tion that companions are paid to endure. Her next enter-
prise, much more congenial to her spirit of independence,
was a school for young girls which she and her friend Fanny Blood conducted with success. She was a rational
woman of unbounded energy, strongly susceptible to
indignation and irascibility, although she never displayed
these latter qualities to her inferiors, to servants, or to
children. Tortured by any position of subordination, she
realized that the position of governess would not be
congenial to her, or to any woman of genius. The odious
post was second only to the position of paid companion to
crotchety wealth. Of governesses she had written (long
before she had met Lady K.), "It is ten to one if they meet
with a reasonable mother; and if she is not so, she will be
continually finding fault to prove she is not ignorant, and
be displeased if her pupils do not improve, but angry if the
proper methods are taken to make them do so. The children treat them with disrespect, and often with in-
solence."[2]

Mary's book did not appear until early the next year,
so that Lady Kingsborough did not have the opportunity
to read it before engaging the author. Had she done so,
she might have thought twice before boasting of her find,
for the book contained in embryo much that Mary was to
expand in her later book, the shrill and notorious *A Vindication of the Rights of Woman*. Mary had a few things
to say about the fine lady who did not nurse her own children, who used rouge and powder, who gave inordinate
attention to her clothes and appearance. One might
think that Lady Kingsborough had sat for the portrait.
She did not suspect that the new governess might prove
to be a calamity in spite of, perhaps because of, her
"philosophic mind."

In October, 1786, Mary arrived in Dublin where she

remained a few days to visit friends and relatives of Fanny Blood. Then, escorted by the Kingsborough butler, she made the trip to Mitchelstown. As she passed through the elaborate gates of the demesne, she felt as though the gates of the Bastille were closing behind her. The letters that she wrote back home to England give a picture of the people and life inside the castle, a picture, it needs to be said, refracted through the genius of a woman who "saw everything on the gloomy side & bestowed censure with a plentiful hand," as her admiring husband wrote of her.[3]

Her first letter to her sister Everina struck the whining note that was to echo and reverberate for a year: "I can scarcely persuade myself that I am awake . . . I have been so very low spirited for some days past, I could not write. All the moments I could spend in solitude were lost in sorrow and unavailing tears . . . I found I was to encounter a host of females—My lady, her stepmother, and three sisters, and *Mrses*. and *Misses* without number, who of course would examine me with the most minute attention . . . I am sure much more is expected from me than I am equal to. With respect to French, I am certain Mr. P[rior] has misled them, and I expect, in consequence of it, to be very much mortified. . . . I hear a fiddle below, the servants are dancing, and the rest of the family are diverting themselves, I only am melancholy and alone."[4]

She duplicated these laments in letters to her publisher: "I have most of the negative comforts of life, yet when weighted with liberty they are of little value. In a christian sense I am resigned—and contented; but it is with pleasure that I observe my declining health, and cherish the hope that I am hastening to the land where all these cares will be forgotten."[5] (Later in life, when the

world had treated her genius with the respect it often pays
to pioneers, she was twice rescued by well-meaning people
from the release she sought in suicide.) But whines extracted from letters give only one dimension. Here, at
greater length, is the letter she wrote to her sister Eliza
on November 5, about a week after her arrival at
Mitchelstown.

"From the date of this you will perceive that I am
arrived at the end of my journey. If I had not dwelt on
the *end* of it—I should have enjoyed it—as the weather
was fine the prospects delightful, and what was of still
more consequence, I had an agreeable companion—a
young Clergyman, who was going to settle in Ireland, in
the same capacity as myself. He was intelligent and had
that kind of politeness, which arises from sensibility. My
conductor, was beyond measure civil and attentive to me,
he is a good sort of a man, I was, at first, at a loss to
guess what department he filled in the family; but I find
he is the Butler, and his wife the house-keeper. I spent
a few days in Dublin, George [Blood] and his mother,
you may suppose, were glad to see me, and so was Betty
Delane. . . ."

Mary admitted that the castle was beautifully situated
near a cloud-capped hill, commanding the type of prospect
she most admired. Yet her spirits were in constant agita-
tion, and she feared herself unequal to her duties as governess. Lady K. she found clever and well disposed, but
not the kind of woman Mary could love. Lord K., whom
she had met but briefly, promised, she thought, nothing
more than good humor and a little unrefined *fun*.

"I have committed to my care three girls," she continued, "the eldest [Margaret] fourteen, by no means
handsome, yet a sweet girl. She has a wonderful capacity,

but she has such a multiplicity of employments it has not room to expand itself, and in all probability will be lost in a heap of rubbish, miscalled accomplishments. I am grieved at being obliged to continue so wrong a system. She is very much afraid of her mother,—that such a creature should be ruled with a rod of iron, when tenderness would lead her anywhere! She is to be always with me. I have just promised to send her love to my sister, so pray receive it. Lady K. is very civil, nay, kind, yet I cannot help fearing her. She has a something in her person and manner which puts me in mind of Mrs. Hewlett—and her turn of thinking seems similar. All the rest of the females labor to be civil to me; but we move in so different a sphere, I feel grateful for their attention; but not amused. I have scarcely a moment to myself to collect my thought and reason sorrow away. When I am alone I endeavour to study the french—and this unwearied application to business undermines my health. I am treated like a gentlewoman—but I cannot easily forget my inferior station—and this something betwixt and between is rather awkward. . . .

"My sweet little girl is now playing and singing to me—she has a good ear and some taste and feeling—I have been interrupted several times since I began this last side. I was going to tell you that my pupils are left to intirely my management—only her Ladyship sometimes condescends to give her opinion. The eldest my favorite has great faults, which I am almost afraid I shall never conquer. The other two are more in a middling way. . . . I intend visiting the poor cabins; as Miss K. is allowed to assist the poor, and I shall make a point of finding them out. Adieu, my dear girl."[6]

2

Lady Kingsborough was thirty-two when she was subjected to Mary's scrutiny and consequent descriptions, which do not tally at all with the treatment later accorded her by *La Belle Assemblée* of January, 1810, wherein she appeared as "the good countess." Mary found her "pretty, always pretty," but a shrewd, clever woman and a great talker, surrounded by dogs on whom she bestowed her caresses and infantine expressions. When her children were ill, she paid them formal visits, and, while Mary endeavored to amuse the children, Lady K. lavished awkward fondness on the dogs. "She rouges," said Mary, "and in short is a fine lady, without fancy or sensibility. I am almost tormented to death by dogs."[7]

"She is very proud," Mary told her sister, "and ready to take fire on the slightest occasion—her temper is violent, and anger intirely dominates in her mind—now, and then, I have seen a momentary start of *tenderness*—sufficient to convince me she might have been a more tolerable companion, had her temper been properly managed; as to her understanding, it could never have been made to rise above mediocrity. I pity her, but I am deprived of all society, and when I do sit with her, she worries me with prejudices, and complaints[8]. . . . Her conversation is ever irksome to me as she has neither sense nor feeling; besides she torments the children. . . .

"To tell the truth she is afraid of me, 'tis not pleasant to be forced to view folly and lament the consequence of it—and yet feel a sort of *mortal* yearning. I love peace—and though the conversation of this female cannot amuse me I try to entertain her—and the result of my endeavors worries *Me* for I have more of her company. She however keeps in her temper surprisingly before me and really labors to be civil. The defect is in her nature. She is devoid of sensibility—of course, *vanity only* inspires her immoderate love of praise—and *selfishness* her traffick of civility—and the fulsome untruths, with all their train of strong expressions without any ideas annexed to them."[9]

The FitzGerald girls, Margaret's aunts, fared no better under the merciless Wollstonecraft pen. They were a "set of silly females" of boisterous spirits, given to meaningless laughter, domestic bickering, and endless discussions on the topics of matrimony and dress. They understood several languages and had read *"cartloads"* of history, but they were incapable of rational conversation and frittered their useless lives away.

"I see Ladies put on rouge without any mauvais honte—," Mary said, "and make up their faces for the day—five hours, and who could do it in less—do many— I assure you, spend in dressing—without including preparations for bed washing with Milk of roses &c &c. . . ."[10] (Mary herself was described years later as a "philosophical sloven" who wore a coarse cloth dress, black worsted stockings, and a beaver hat, "with her hair hanging lank about her shoulders.") "You cannot conceive my dear Girl the dissipated lives the women of quality lead—when I am in spirits I will give you a faithful picture. In many respects the *Great* and *little* vulgar resemble and in none more than the motives which induce them to marry. They look not for a companion, and are seldom alone together but in bed. The husband, perhaps drunk and the wife's head full of the *pretty* compliment that some creature, that nature designed for a man—paid her at the card table."[11]

There were a few in the household who did not supply heat for the distillation of Mary's venom. The Right Honorable George Ogle was one of these. It was not because he was right honorable or M.P. for Wexford that

Mary esteemed him—these distinctions he would have had to overcome. He succeeded with Mary because he was "a *genius*, and *unhappy*" and the author of sentimental poems, such as "Banna's Banks" and "Molly Asthore." She found him a rational man of sensibility, and he found that distress made her "interesting." It is hard to believe that Mrs. Ogle and her sister, Miss Moore, who were also in Mary's favor, were any more intelligent or civil than the Kingsboroughs, but they had the initial advantage of not being Mary's employers, and she was not dependent upon their caprice. Actually Mary was in an enviable post. She was a great favorite with the family (upon her own admission), all labored to be civil to her, and all showed interest and pride in her wit and conversation. Mary herself was a most determined woman, and she showed great determination to be tiresome. So it seemed to Lady K.

The favorite place in Mary's heart was held by her eldest pupil, Margaret, tall for her age, blue-eyed, afraid of her mother, longing for affection. Mary's first impression was that the children were, literally speaking, wild Irish, unformed and not very pleasing. Yet in less than a week she had discovered that Margaret was sweet, if by no means as handsome as her younger sister Caroline. Her mother did not appreciate her "wonderful capacity," but set up harsh restrictions, such as one against reading novels, which Mary removed when the pupils were left to her management.

Not that Margaret was without faults, great faults that Mary thought she would never conquer: a violence of temper inherited from her mother, a precocious recognition of her mother's faults (what pupil of Mary's could not perceive them?), and cleverness at mimicry and ridicule. The misery that Mary was determined to endure in the company of the adults was almost compensated for by the children. "I go to the nursery," she wrote, "something like maternal fondness fills my bosom. The children cluster about me—one catches a kiss, another lisps my long name—while a sweet little boy, who is conscious that he is a favorite, calls himself my Tom. At the sight of their mother they tremble and run to me for protection —this renders them dear to me—and I discover the kind of happiness I was formed to enjoy."[12]

3

We can learn from Mary's writings, particularly her *Thoughts on the Education of Daughters* and the later *Vindication of the Rights of Woman,* the educational philosophy to which Margaret was exposed as Mary's proselyte and which was to guide the remainder of Margaret's life. The books might be interpreted as reprimands to the Kingsboroughs (there is one specific portrait of Lady K. in *The Rights of Woman*), as well as reprimands to most writers on the subject of woman, one of whom felt the supreme womanly virtue to be "a propensity to melt into affectionate sorrow." Another writer, Dr. John Gregory, had advised his daughters, "if you happen to have any learning, keep it a profound secret, especially from the men, who generally look with a jealous and malignant eye on a woman of great parts, and a cultivated understanding."[13] In France Rousseau had given his opinion: "La femme est faite pour plaire et pour être subjugée."

Mary felt that the grand blessing of life, the basis of every virtue, and the source of true grace could be found in independence. This happy state could be achieved only through the cultivation of the understanding, a faculty in which she had a pathetic faith. Love itself should not be allowed to dethrone the superior powers of the mind or usurp the scepter of the understanding; she was "very far from thinking love irresistible, and not to be conquered." On looking about her Mary saw silly women anxious to inspire love when they should be exacting respect; using the artifices of red, blue, and yellow powder along with cunning and coquetry to ensnare husbands; visiting to display finery; playing cards and dancing, not to mention spending their mornings trifling. While they retained some beauty they remained their husband's mistresses, only to be driven from the "throne of beauty" by their own daughters; had these women taken a seat on the "bench of reason" they would have remained their husbands' companions forever. Such women who neglect the potentialities of the understanding discover too late that "even the lustre of their eyes, and the flippant sportiveness of refined coquetry, will not always secure them attention during a whole evening. . . ." They "only inspire love."

Such is Nature's wise ordering of things that women who suckle their children preserve their own health and find that there is such a natural interval between the birth of each child that we should seldom see a houseful of babes. (Lady K. had twelve.) "Cold would be the heart of a husband . . . who did not feel more delight at seeing his child suckled by its mother than the most artful wanton tricks could ever raise. . . ." (Lady K. turned her children over to hirelings at birth.) Yet there are many husbands so devoid of sense and affection that "during the first effervescence of voluptuous fondness" they refuse to allow their wives to suckle.

Silly mothers cause their daughters to devote the first years of their lives to acquiring a smattering of "accomplishments"; girls learn something of music, drawing, and geography. "If they can play over a few tunes to their acquaintance, and have a drawing or two (half done by the master) to hang up in their rooms, they imagine themselves artists for the rest of their lives."[14] While these ornaments are being painfully acquired, strength of mind and body, reason and understanding are sacrificed to libertine notions of beauty, beauty which can do nothing but find husbands for the girls.

Instead of cultivating female follies, the wise mother will see to the management of the temper, the first and most important branch of education. Rich and poor should attend the same school and dress alike to prevent any of the distinctions of vanity. The very youngest children should be introduced "as a kind of show" to botany, mechanics, astronomy, reading, writing, arithmetic, natural history, and natural philosophy, the elements of religion, history, the history of man, and politics, although these pursuits should never encroach on gymnastic plays in the open air. It is an indignity against the rights of women to send boys out into the air for exercise and to confine girls in a stuffy schoolroom.

After children have applied themselves to these studies until they have ripened to the age of nine, young people of superior abilities or fortune may go on to study the living and dead languages, science, history, politics, and polite literature. Women should be taught the elements of anatomy and medicine, not only to enable them to take proper care of their own health, but to make them rational nurses of their infants, parents, and husbands. Women might certainly study the art of healing, and be physicians as well as nurses.

4

Mary's methods of teaching may be gathered from a little book she published soon after she left the Kingsboroughs' service: *Original Stories from Real Life; with Conversations, Calculated to Regulate the Affections, and Form the Mind to Truth and Goodness.*[15] The characters of the book are Mrs. Mason, a widow, and her two charges, Mary and Caroline. There seems to be no reason to believe that the "Real Life" of the title does not mean what it says: Mrs. Mason is Mary Wollstonecraft, Mary is Margaret, and Caroline is Margaret's sister Caroline. Mary may or may not have possessed the virtues attributed to Mrs. Mason, but Margaret and Caroline certainly did possess in real life the faults attributed to them in fiction. The introduction to the book, with due alteration of details, sets the scene in the Kingsborough household:

Mary and Caroline, though the children of wealthy parents, were, in their infancy, left entirely to the management of servants, or people equally ignorant. Their mother died suddenly, and their father, who found them very troublesome at home, placed them under the tuition of a woman of tenderness and discernment, a near relation, who was induced to take on herself the important charge through motives of compassion [not for the salary of a governess].

They were shamefully ignorant, considering that Mary had been fourteen, and Caroline twelve years in the world. If they had been merely ignorant, the task would not have appeared so arduous; but they had caught every prejudice that the vulgar casually instill. In order to eradicate these prejudices, and substitute good habits instead of those they had carelessly contracted, Mrs. Mason never suffered them to be out of her sight. They were allowed to ask questions on all occasions, a method she would not have adopted, had she educated them from the first according to the suggestions of her own reason, to which experience had given its sanction.

They had tolerable capacities; but Mary had a turn for ridicule, and Caroline was vain of her person. She was, indeed, very handsome, and the inconsiderate encomiums that had, in her presence, been lavished on her beauty made her, even at that early age, affected.

Mrs. Mason strikes the modern reader as an energetic, confident, impeccable, rational, uncompromising, arid, and heartless drillmaster. Relentlessly she instructs the children in the principles of all the virtues including "the inconveniences of immoderate indulgence" and kindness to servants and animals. Most of her stories contain moral lines, which we hope were more successful with the King girls than they would be with any pair of modern children.

Mrs. Mason's ideal woman was not Lady Sly (or Lady K.?) with her fine carriage and beautiful horses, her elegantly liveried servants, her mansion with lofty rooms hung with silk, her pleasure gardens well laid out with trees and shrubs, summerhouses and temples. "This is *state*," Mrs. Mason tells the girls, "not *dignity*." Nearer the ideal was Mrs. Trueman, the curate's wife, sweetly voiced, easily mannered, simply dressed; or Anna Lofty, the schoolmistress daughter of a nobleman in reduced circumstances, who preferred poverty and honest work to "swelling the train of the proud or vicious great."

One of the most striking examples of pedagogical precept, this one from the *Rights of Woman*, instructs parents how to elicit rational obedience from their children: "It is your interest to obey me [says the prudent mother to her child] till you can judge for yourself; and the Almighty Father of all has implanted an affection in me to serve as a guard to you whilst your reason is unfolding; but when your mind arrives at maturity, you must only obey me, or rather respect my opinions, so far as they coincide with the light that is breaking in on your own mind."[16] Harsh and ineffective as all this sounds, it worked. Margaret never ceased to love Mary, her own Mrs. Mason, and for the remainder of her life she attempted to follow the precepts of her governess. The fourteen-year-old counterpart of Margaret in *Original Stories* was impressed enough to say, "I wish to be a woman and to be like Mrs. Mason."

5

When Mary first arrived at Mitchelstown Castle she did not see much of Lady Kingsborough, who was confined to her room with a sore throat, although she did see half a dozen of her companions—"I mean not her children, but her dogs."[17] By the time Lady K. was well again, all the children were ill, and Mary herself was suffering from a nervousness that left her nearly fainting. Yet her incredible energy kept her going, teaching the children, studying French, displaying her wit in the drawing room, and visiting the poor cabins.

It may be presumed that Mary and the girls, like Mrs. Mason of *Original Stories*, dressed tactfully while visiting the poor lest they give offense. The scene can be reconstructed and the wisdom of the visits questioned. How judicious was it of a noblewoman to allow her three daughters to visit the most wretched hovels in Europe in the company of so radical a person as Mary Wollstonecraft? The contrast between the tall chambers of the castle and the squalid, mean dwellings of the poor would be apparent to any little girls. But the question why this inequality should exist might not enter their eighteenth-century heads. Mary asked the question a few years later in fanatic sympathy for the French Revolution. Perhaps it is safe to say that Margaret's republicanism dated from these visits.

The winter of 1786-87 passed slowly for Mary, if not for Margaret, who, for the first time, was under the care of a woman she could respect and love and on whom she could indulge her crush. In December, Margaret came down with a violent fever, perhaps diphtheria, and could not bear to have Mary out of her sight. Her life was despaired of, the despair producing an intimacy among the Kingsboroughs that was apparent even to the gloomy Mary. Margaret survived, but she remained weak and ailing for almost a year. "The fever was prematurely stopped," Mary wrote in March of the next year, "and it was of so malignant a nature, the remnant of it still lurks in her blood, and produces very disagreeable effects. My anxiety on her account is very much augmented by her Mother's improper treatment—as I fear she will hurry her into a consumption—and I dread it the more as it is a disorder incident to the family."[18]

Early in February, Mary and the children left Mitchelstown for Dublin. The Kingsboroughs and Fitz-Geralds followed a few days later, moving into two separate town houses. Mary had better apartments in Lord Kingsborough's house on Henrietta Street: a room of her own (a larger tent in which to sulk), a fine schoolroom, the use of a drawing room with a harpsichord, and a parlor in which to receive her male visitors. Immediately there was an inundation of masters for the children and the hurly-burly of society for the adults. The children applied themselves to the French, German, and Italian lessons, and Mary had more time to herself. She was no longer "confined to the society of silly females," but soon her complaint was that she was "confined to the society of children." There was almost always antagonism between her and Lady Kingsborough, but it is impossible to feel, even though the source of information is Mary's letters, that Mary herself was not at fault.

Again and again Lady Kingsborough attempted to see that Mary was amused; she appears to have been proud of Mary's conversational powers and to have made every effort to stop her sulking in her room and to get her into the drawing room. Together they went to church, to the theater, to a Handel commemoration, to a masquerade, to the Rotunda. But Mary had set her heart upon being slighted. "You know," she wrote to her sister, "I never liked Lady K., but I find her still more haughty and disagreeable now she is not under Mrs. Fitz-Gerald's eye. Indeed, she behaved so improperly to me once, or twice, in the Drawing room, I determined never to go into it again. I could not bear to stalk in to be stared at, and her *proud* condescension added to my embarrassment. I begged to be excused in a civil way—but she would not allow me to absent myself. I had too, another reason, the expence of hair-dressing, and millinery, would have exceeded the sum I chuse to spend in those things. I was determined—just at this juncture she offered me a present, a poplin gown and petticoat, I refused it, and explained myself—she was very angry; but Mrs. F. who was consulted on the occasion, took my part, and made her ask my pardon, and consent to let me stay always in my own room. Since that she has endeavoured to treat me with more propriety, and I believe she does so to the best of her knowledge."[19]

Three weeks later Lady Kingsborough was entertaining her father-in-law, old Lord Kingston, at dinner. When the ladies left the dining room, Lady K., Mrs. Ogle, and Miss Moore dropped in on Mary in her room where they found her brooding in a melancholy mood.

All three ladies urged Mary to come down to the drawing room to meet Lord Kingston. It is impossible to think that Lady K. was motivated by anything but good will. "I at last consented," Mary wrote, "and could perceive that [Lady K.] had a guard over herself—For to tell you a secret she is afraid of me. Why she wishes to keep me I cannot guess—for she cannot bear that any one should take notice of me. Nay would you believe it she used several arts to get me out of the room before the gentlemen came up [having invited Mary down purposely to meet Lord Kingston]—one of them I really wanted to see [was] Mr. Ogle—He is between forty and fifty—a *genius*, and *unhappy*. Such a man you may suppose would catch your sister's eye. As he has the name of being a man of sense Lady K. has chosen him for her *flirt*—don't mistake me—her flirtations are very harmless and she can neither understand nor relish his conversation. But she wishes to be taken particular notice of by a man of *acknowledged* cleverness. As he had not seen me lately he came and seated himself by me—indeed his sensibility has ever led him to pay attention to a poor forlorn stranger. He paid me some *fanciful* compliments—and lent me some very pretty stanzas—melancholy ones, you may suppose, as he thought they would accord with my feelings. Lord K. came up—and was surprised at seeing me *there*—he bowed respectfully—a concatenation of thoughts made me out *blush* her Ladyship's rouge."[20] Poor Lady Kingsborough could find no way to please her governess, who brooded over the imagined slights for years until she purged herself by writing *The Rights of Woman*.

Early in the summer the family went to England, first to Bristol Hot Wells and then to Bath. There is not much mention of Margaret in the letters Mary continued to write except for an occasional statement that she was "very far from being well." The children continued their studies, the parents took the baths, and Mary found therapy in writing her first novel. In the early autumn the family was in London. Mary had persuaded them to make a trip to the Continent, and she was granted a few days to pay a visit to her sister, whom she had not seen for over a year. As Mary was preparing to leave, Margaret showed so much regret at being separated from her that Lady Kingsborough flew into a passion and dismissed Mary on the spot. "I long since imagined that my departure would be sudden," Mary wrote to her sister on November 7. The next week the Kingsboroughs left London, not for the Continent, but for Mitchelstown.

But they were not yet finished with Mary, or, rather, she was not yet finished with them. She had the joy of putting a portrait of Lady Kingsborough into her *Rights of Woman.* "And she who takes her dogs to bed," Mary wrote, "and nurses them with a parade of sensibility, when sick, will suffer her babes to grow up crooked in a nursery. This illustration of my argument is drawn from a matter of fact. The woman whom I allude to was handsome, reckoned very handsome, by those who do not miss the mind when the face is plump and fair; but her understanding had not been led from female duties by literature, nor her innocence debauched by knowledge. No, she was quite feminine, according to the masculine acceptation of the word; and, so far from loving these spoiled brutes that filled the place which her children ought to have occupied, she only lisped out a pretty mixture of French and English nonsense, to please the men who flocked round her. The wife, mother, and human creature, were all swallowed up by the factitious character which an improper education and the selfish vanity of beauty had produced."[21]

We must believe that Lady K. read the lines, for the

book became notorious and was read on all sides. One can imagine that she felt some of the same rage she had previously felt when she dismissed Mary. Margaret was, of course, Mary's complete proselyte, but Lady Kingsborough did not remain uninfluenced. The lisping, silly, simpering female whom Mary described, ironically prided herself later in life on her understanding. In 1806, the Honorable Mrs. Calvert wrote in her diary: "How Lady Kingston does talk! And poor woman, how excellent does she think her own understanding and judgment. She really does not want for good sense, but by overvaluing it so much, one does not give her credit even for what she possesses."[22]

Margaret and her governess seem never to have met again, but they corresponded. A year after she left the Kingsboroughs Mary wrote, "I had, the other day, the satisfaction of again receiving from my poor, dear Margaret. With all a mother's fondness I could transcribe a part of it. She says, every day her affections to me, and dependence on heaven increases, &c. I miss her innocent caresses—and sometimes indulge a pleasing hope that she may be allowed to cheer my childless age—if I am to live to be old."[23]

MARGARET, LADY MOUNT CASHELL

CHAPTER **3.**

WE DO NOT KNOW what governess was engaged to take
the place of Mary Wollstonecraft, but it is safe to surmise
that she was a woman of less philosophic mind, less
obtrusive, and more able to conceal any resentment she
may have felt. Margaret continued under the Wollstonecraft influence, showing an unfashionable contempt for
"the usual objects of female vanity," attempting to correct
the faults that Mary had pointed out, and cultivating her
understanding. She herself tells us that at seventeen
(two years after Mary had left her) she was more
flattered by a compliment to her understanding from an
old clergyman than by any homage to her beauty from
fashionable young men. One fashionable young man with
whom she carried on a "mild flirtation" was Charles
Kendal Bushe, five years her senior, and later Chief
Justice of the King's Bench in Ireland.[1] His father, the
Reverend Thomas Bushe, held the chaplaincy at Kingston
College.

Lady Kingsborough recovered from her year of purgatory with Mary and continued the life of a lady of fashion:
winter in Mitchelstown, spring in Dublin, summer at Bath,
and autumn in London. Neither she nor her guests
showed the same disdain for dress and display that Mary

had implanted in Margaret. *Walker's Hibernian Magazine* for April, 1790, was pleased to report that "Lady Kingsborough gave a superb rout, ball, and supper at her house in Henrietta Street, to a very numerous party of the nobility and gentry. The entertainment was perfectly magnificent, taste being in it united with expence. At this splendid party the Countess of Westmorland [wife of John Fane, the newly appointed Lord Lieutenant of Ireland] appeared in an entire dress of Brussels lace laid over a pink Irish satin, the estimated expence of which exceeded 500 [pounds]." The previous month the *Hibernian* had been equally pleased to report that the dress had been ordered: "This is reviving the real magnificence of dress which should be adapted to the splendour of a Court, and to the dignity of station."

The next public notice is one of importance. The *Gentlemen's Magazine* announced a marriage on September 12, 1791, "At the seat of her father, at Mitchelstown in Ireland, the Hon. Miss King, eldest daughter of Lord Kingsborough to the Earl of Mount Cashell of Moore Park." In many respects, Margaret could not ask for a better husband. Stephen Moore, second Earl of Mount Cashell, was twenty-one, handsome, gentle, and easy tempered. More amiable than clever, he had received almost no education and had attended no university, but he was beloved by all who knew him, especially by his subordinates who could wheedle him out of anything. His seat, Moore Park, was at Kilworth, in the County Cork, about seven miles from Mitchelstown.

The Mount Cashell family descended from Richard Moore, a glover at Barnstaple in England, who settled at Clonmel in the County Tipperary in 1655. He was a shrewd and industrious merchant, so prosperous that his son was able to purchase the estate at Kilworth in the year 1684 for the sum of £5,500. This son was personally known to King William III, to whom he lent £3,000 which was never repaid, although William appointed him governor of the County Tipperary and colonel of its militia. His grandson, Stephen Moore, was created Baron Kilworth in 1764 and Viscount Mount Cashell in 1766; the viscount was succeeded by his second son, Stephen, who was created Earl of Mount Cashell in 1781 and who married Helen, daughter of the second Earl of Moira. When the first Earl of Mount Cashell died in 1790, his son, Lord Kilworth, was on his travels, but he returned at once to Ireland to assume the responsibilities of the second Earl of Mount Cashell and to marry the daughter of his nearest noble neighbor, Lord Kingsborough.

The bare journal announcement of the marriage in the *Gentlemen's Magazine* can only suggest the ceremony by which the Honorable Margaret King became at nineteen the Countess of Mount Cashell. By an Act of Parliament in Ireland in the seventeenth and eighteenth years of the reign of His Majesty George III, Lord and Lady Kingsborough had been empowered to levy £23,000 on their estates in Ireland, and now they took advantage of that act to apply £6,000 "to the advancement and for the portion" of their daughter Margaret.[2] If the Kingsboroughs provided their eldest daughter with the ceremonies that other Irish noblemen provided, and there is no reason to believe that they did not, the guests were treated to tragedies and comedies, balls and concerts, perhaps a *fête champêtre*. Orders were given that Mitchelstown should be made especially neat and clean; troops and artillery were stationed on the route that the young couple took on the way to their honeymoon.

The wars in France prevented Lord M. from taking his bride to the Continent, but the great Irish families always had one foot in London, and we can assume that the Mount Cashells went there at least and that Lady Mount Cashell appeared at court and in the fashionable houses of London society. Upon their return to Kilworth, Lady Mount Cashell became mistress of her husband's principal seat, Moore Park, a spacious rather than elegant mansion in a richly wooded demesne of eight hundred acres. The river Funcheon, well stocked with trout and salmon, flowed through the demesne, pursuing a winding course through a channel skirted by limestone rocks. Within the demesne was the ancient seat of the Condons, Cloghleagh Castle, a lofty square tower situated on the highest ground on the bank of the river and commanding one of its most important passes.

Kilworth, a market and post town at the foot of the Kilworth Mountains, was a less elegant, less planned village than Mitchelstown. It consisted of one long irregular street with some three hundred houses, an ancient church, a Catholic chapel, a neat market house, a glebe house, and three detached glebes amounting to fifteen acres. The Honorable and Reverend Robert Moore, the incumbent, had cure of the souls. Most of the people were, of course, Catholics, and their spiritual life was directed by the Reverend John Bourke, D.D., who, like most Irish priests, also provided leadership other than spiritual. In the village the Catholics had a Classical School that attracted students from all parts, the poor scholars being boarded free in the farmers' houses, where they instructed the family in return.

Lady Mount Cashell took over her duties as mistress of Moore Park with the "silly project of governing" her husband. Amiable as he was, his personality clashed with hers: his aversion to literature had to contend with her principal recreation, reading; his respect for wealth and

titles was offset by her own simplicity of living; in the
House of Lords he was a Tory, at home his wife was a
United Irishwoman; he preferred the society of nobles
and gentry, she sought out and applauded every radical
and freethinker she could find; he (descendant of the
Barnstaple glover) resented any expenditure for the
education of his children, she looked upon education and
the development of the understanding as the chief re-
sponsibility of a parent.

The family lived principally in the country at Moore
Park, but when the House of Lords was in session they
moved to Mount Cashell House, one of the finest resi-
dences on St. Stephen's Green in Dublin, and sometimes
they made a trip to London. Lady Mount Cashell's chief
interests were in her children (whom she nursed herself),
in liberal politics, in medicine, and in literature. As bride
and mother she was still the pupil of Mary Wollstonecraft.

From the beginning of her wedded life there was,
inevitably, quarreling. Had she been content to use the
ordinary female bag of tricks, she might have been able
to govern her husband at least as well as the grooms and
housekeepers who flattered his lordship until their will
was his. But Lady M., vindicated by the *Rights of
Woman*, refused to compromise, to use "lofty tones" or
"wheedling accents." The strain between the couple continued and there was some talk of a separation, but such a
possibility was reduced by the arrival of the children.
Their first child, Stephen, was born in Dublin on August
20, 1792. Then came

> Robert, July 11, 1793
> Helena Eleanor, March 3, 1795
> Jane Eliza, September 17, 1796
> Edward George, August 18, 1798

Richard Francis Stanislas, July 26, 1802
Elizabeth Anne, August 27, 1804

An eighth child, Francis, who was born on October 28, 1800, died young.

2

The Mount Cashells were in London late in 1794, the time of the trial of Thomas Hardy, John Horne Tooke, and John Thelwall for high treason. The only offense the men had committed was the attempt to assemble a general convention of the people for the purpose of obtaining parliamentary reform. English air was charged with the fear of revolution, but the jury commendably refused to convict the accused. A few days after the acquittal, Lady M., with her passion for seeing all the extraordinary men of her day, walked into Hardy's shoemaking shop. Hardy was absent, but Lady M. explained to his wife that she wanted to order a pair of shoes from the man who had been acquitted of high treason. The wife said that he would return presently, and, knocking Lady M. on the arm, she pointed to a little, vulgar, dirty man and whispered, "There's another of them."

"Are you not one of those who were committed to the Tower?" Lady M. said to Hardy, upon his return.

"Yes, I had that honor," he replied with great calmness.

Lady M. was delighted with the reply and ordered a pair of shoes forthwith; but, when she received them and put them on, she found that they were shockingly made, pinching and galling her dreadfully. She took a hackney coach to his house and said to him, "Mr. Hardy, I am very sorry for it but my feet are democratical and your shoes are aristocratical, and they don't agree at all. Pray have the kindness to put them on the last for me."

Hardy made her a new pair, which, though bad shoes, did not hurt. He refused payment for either pair and was pleased, upon asking her name, to know that his gift had been frankly accepted by a countess.[3]

3

Meanwhile, Lady Kingsborough had separated from her husband and taken a small cottage in Windsor, where she lived with her young daughter, Mary Elizabeth. The Honorable Mrs. Calvert called on her there in 1794 before going to Ireland, and they took a walk on Windsor Terrace one evening, accompanied by Mrs. Calvert's four-year-old son, Felix. "The sweet fellow attracted the attention of the King, who was there, and he talked to him for an hour," Mrs. Calvert wrote in her journal. "So pleased was His Majesty with his appearance and conversation, that he begged I would bring him the next evening to the Terrace, as he wished to show him to the Queen and Princesses."[4] Mrs. Calvert paid another visit in May of 1797, a few days after the marriage of the Princess Royal to the Duke of Würtemberg. The two ladies again walked on the Terrace in the evening and met the Royal Family, who stopped to speak to them. The ladies thought that the Duchess of Würtemberg looked very happy, leaning on her husband.

Back in Mitchelstown, Lord Kingsborough, now a man of forty and the father of twelve, consoled himself by taking a mistress, Miss Eliner Hallenan, who bore him two children.

Lady Mount Cashell's six living brothers, their educations completed, began their life's work. The eldest, Big George, had nothing on earth to do after finishing his studies at Oxford but wait lazily to inherit the estates and become third Earl of Kingston. The remaining five brothers went into the Army, the Navy, the diplomatic service, or the Church. One evening Big George, in his idleness, was walking on the promenade of St. Stephen's Green by moonlight with Miss Johnstone, when the following conversation took place, as Lady Mount Cashell reported it years later to Claire Clairmont:

"What a fine night to run away with another man's wife," said Big George.

"And why not another man's daughter?" said Miss Johnstone.

"Will you?" said he.

"Yes," said she.

"Done," said Big George, taking her hand.

"Done," said Miss Johnstone, giving him hers.[5]

That very night, without further courtship, they ran away and settled in the British West Indies, where they had three children.[6] Eventually Big George was persuaded to return to Ireland and to marry in 1794 Lady Helena Moore, sister of Lord Mount Cashell.

4

Upon leaving the Kingsboroughs, Mary Wollstonecraft decided to devote herself to literature. Liberals and radicals received her work with extravagant praise, whereas equally articulate conservatives thought her "a hyena in petticoats." In 1792 she went to Paris in order to observe the progress of the French Revolution. There she lived through the Reign of Terror and met Captain Gilbert Imlay, an American, to whom she bore a daughter, Fanny Imlay. Imlay sent Mary on business to Norway, and in her letters from Norway she wrote that Dublin was the most hospitable city that she had ever visited. Returning to England, she was shunned by Imlay, who offered her an annuity which she scornfully refused with the words

"I am not sufficiently humbled to depend on your benef-
icence." Yet in her despair she attempted to drown herself by leaping from Putney Bridge after having walked
up and down in the rain so that her clothes would become
thoroughly soaked and not prevent her sinking.

In 1796 she met William Godwin, the leading London
radical, and a friendship sprang up between them. When
they discovered that Mary was pregnant they married,
although both were theoretically opposed to such bour-
geois slavery. Their daughter, Mary, afterwards the wife
of Percy Shelley, was born at the end of August, 1797,
and Mrs. William Godwin died ten days later. She had in
mind two projects which she did not live to undertake:
one was a series of books for children, the other a book on
the physical education of children for mothers.

William Godwin appears to have been a pedantic,
humorless man, the social antithesis of Mary Wollstonecraft, mistress of wit and sally. But to Mary and the
liberally inclined he was a conspicuous philosopher, the
author of *Political Justice* who could think no wrong.
Three years after Mary's death he visited Ireland on the
invitation of John Philpot Curran, the popular Irish wit
and liberal politician. Curran wrote to Godwin from
Dublin in June, 1800: "There are many here that know
you in print, and are much pleased with the hope I have
given them of knowing you in person. One of them,
Lady Mountcashel, who is now settled in Dublin for the
summer, speaks of you with peculiar regard, mixed with
a tender and regretful retrospect to past times and to past
events with which you have yourself been connected."[7]

In July, Godwin was in Dublin, recording in his
journal and in his letters several dinners with Lady Mount
Cashell—Lord M. not being mentioned—and an especially impressive excursion in her cabriolet to the Devil's

Glen. The description of her he sent back to England was not kindhearted. "Lady Mountcashel is a singular character," he wrote, "a democrat and a republican in all their sternness, yet with no ordinary portion either of understanding or good nature. If any of our comic writers were to fall in her company, the infallible consequence would be her being gibbetted in a play. She is uncommonly tall and brawny, with bad teeth, white eyes, and a handsome countenance. She commonly dresses, as I have seen Mrs. Fenwick dressed out of poverty, with a grey gown, and no linen visible; but with gigantic arms, which she commonly folds, naked and exposed almost up to the shoulders."[8]

Back in England Godwin began a correspondence with Lady M. and at once charged her with not behaving with sufficient tenderness toward her children, although he gave her no specific examples of untenderness. She was some time in replying, for she had been disabled by a dangerous fall from her horse; but when she did reply, on April 6, 1801, she did not plead guilty. At that time she was at Moore Park taking full charge of the children herself because Mr. Murphy, the boys' tutor, did not go into the country when the family left Dublin. No person, she wrote to Godwin, could be more thoroughly aware of the baneful effects of tyranny on young minds, and had it not been her "peculiar good fortune to meet with the extraordinary woman to whose superior penetration & affectionate mildness of manner" she attributed whatever virtues she possessed, she would have become "a most ferocious animal."[9]

She welcomed Godwin's advice on the education of her children, presuming that he was equipped to give advice, and agreed that a combination of public and private education was judicious, especially for boys, although she did not suppose it would be in her power to follow that plan with her own. (Lord M. had something to say regarding how much money should be spent on education.) Young as her children were, she perceived in them a diversity of character which required a difference in treatment.

Thus in plain living and high thinking passed the early married years of the pupil of Mary Wollstonecraft, enthusiastic female. While her mother was chatting with royalty on Windsor Terrace, she was visiting the shop of a radical shoemaker accused of high treason. While her husband was sitting in the Irish House of Lords, she was entertaining such liberals as Grattan, Curran, and (Lord M. not being present) William Godwin.

CHAPTER 4.

IN THE FALL OF 1797 high and low in London were talking and speculating about the following notice which appeared in *The True Briton* and other London newspapers on Saturday, September 23:

YOUNG LADY ELOPED

Whereas a young lady went from her Mother's House near Windsor, on Sunday Evening the 3d inst. and has not since been heard of, except by a letter of Wednesday the 6th inst. having the post mark Windsor upon it.

The Lady is about 17 years old, clear brown complexion, with very dark brown hair, light blue eyes, Grecian nose, long oval face, is about 5 feet 5 inches high, rather slim made, and a pretty elegant figure; speaks with a little lisp, and rather quick.

Whoever will give information of the place of abode of the Young Lady, so that she may be restored to her Family and Friends, shall receive a Reward of ONE HUNDRED GUINEAS, by applying to Mr. Lowten, in the Temple.

The notice was repeated in the newspapers until September 29, when *The True Briton* announced that "The Young Lady who has been advertised as having eloped from her

friends, was recovered in consequence of Habeas Corpus."
The Young Lady was the Honorable Mary Elizabeth
King, daughter of Lord Kingsborough.

Lady Kingsborough's contentment near the royal
family was changed to consternation on the Sunday evening when her beloved daughter walked out of the house
at Windsor, not to return. A note Mary left on her
dressing table saying that she was about to throw herself
into the Thames produced a state of shock in Lady Kingsborough, who did not know which way to turn. When her
servants dragged the river near the house, they found a
bonnet and shawl upon the bank; but on Wednesday a
letter from Mary assured her mother that she was at least
alive. The only male relative near by was Lady Kingsborough's illegitimate half-brother, Colonel Henry Gerard
FitzGerald, who lived at Bishopgate up the Thames with
his wife (the daughter of Sir Robert Staples)[1] and their
two children. Colonel FitzGerald seemed beside himself
at the loss of his cousin and did what he could, which was
not much really; he could do nothing more effectual than
call on Lady Kingsborough daily and make inquiries as to
whether any intelligence had been received. The Kingsborough men, who were in Ireland, were notified at once.

It was not until the arrival of Lord Kingsborough and
his second son, Colonel Robert King, recently returned
from the wars in America, that definite action was taken.
Three weeks after Mary's disappearance, notices appeared
in the newspapers and placards were posted all over London offering a reward for any information which would
lead to the recovery of the missing girl. By this time
Londoners knew her identity and talked of nothing else at
their dinner tables.

The first bit of intelligence came from a postboy who
called on Lord Kingsborough to say that while he was

taking a gentleman in a post chaise to London, he saw a young lady walking by herself upon the road. The gentleman ordered him to stop and offered the young lady a seat, which she accepted without any hesitation. When they reached London, the young lady and the gentleman went away together.

On Wednesday, the twenty-seventh, a servant girl who thought she might have some information called on Lady Kingsborough. Her parents kept a rooming house on Clayton Street, near Kennington Turnpike, to which a gentleman brought a young lady on the preceding Sunday. He slept with her that night until six-thirty in the morning when he left, not to return. The young lady had sent the servant girl out for a newspaper and remarked that the description of the missing girl resembled herself somewhat. The description made reference to the young lady's long hair, and the servant became most suspicious when she came upon her new roomer in the act of cutting off her own hair, which was unusually long.

While the girl was telling her exciting story to the Kingsboroughs, the door of the apartment opened and in walked Colonel FitzGerald to pay his daily visit of sympathy. He did not notice the servant, but she noticed him and wide-eyed exclaimed, "Why there's the very gentleman who visits the young lady!" Confounded, Colonel FitzGerald ran from the apartment.

Mr. Lowten was at once dispatched to Clayton Street, only to learn that the young lady was out looking for fresh lodgings. When she returned she at first refused to go with Mr. Lowten, but, upon his assurance that her refusal was in vain, she gave him her hand; he handed her into his carriage and took her to her father's house in Great George Street, Hanover Square. Mary was confined there, with her hair cropped, until it was possible to

take her to Mitchelstown.   At Mitchelstown she could live
in quiet retirement, safe from prying London eyes, as her
hair grew long again.

The indignation of the Kingsboroughs was intensified
by the ingratitude of Colonel FitzGerald, who, though
illegitimate, had been raised as a member of the family and
owed his commission to the gracious liberality of Lord
Kingsborough.   Colonel Robert King sought him out and
with some difficulty found him.   On the last day of September a challenge was delivered by Major Robert Wood,
Colonel King's second.   Colonel FitzGerald said that he
himself would be unable to find a second, on account of the
odium thrown on his character, but that he was sensible
of Major Wood's honor and that he would meet Colonel
King the next day without a second of his own.   The next
morning, which was Sunday, October 1, they met near the
Magazine in Hyde Park, FitzGerald being accompanied
only by a surgeon, who refused to act as second.   The
combatants exchanged six shots at ten paces.   After the
fourth shot FitzGerald asked Major Wood's advice as a
friend.   Major Wood replied that he was no friend of
his, though a friend to humanity, and that if FitzGerald
acknowledged that he was the vilest of human beings and
would bear without reply any language from Colonel
King, however harsh, then the duel would be at an end.
Colonel FitzGerald acknowledged that he had acted
wrongly, but no more.   Colonel King did not consider the
reply satisfactory.   After two more shots Colonel Fitz-
Gerald's powder and balls were expended, and an agreement was made that the duel would be resumed on Monday morning.   The Duke of York, however, heard of
the affair and immediately ordered Colonel Stephens of
the Guards to put the two duellists under arrest.   On
Thursday Lord Kingsborough wrote a terse note to Fitz-

Gerald telling him that if he ever came within reach again the consequences would be fatal.[2]

The discovery, the confinement, the cropped hair, and the duel, in accomplishing their immediate aims, did nothing to kill the love which Mary had for her cousin. Lord Kingsborough dismissed a serving maid whom he discovered to be an accomplice of the lovers, but in her dismissal she carried a letter from Mary, the contents of which were enough to induce Colonel FitzGerald to follow his beloved to Ireland at the risk of his life. Lord Kingsborough was absent from Mitchelstown when FitzGerald put up there, in disguise, at the King's Arms, a hotel near the gates of the demesne kept by an old retainer of the family named Barry. Barry was suspicious when he observed that his mysterious guest remained indoors during the day and left the inn every night. Lord Kingsborough was expected at Fermoy for an examination of the militia, and there Barry went with his intelligence. At once Lord Kingsborough and Colonel King rode to Mitchelstown to be told that the mysterious stranger had left that morning. A postboy was able to inform them that the stranger had gone to Kilworth and was staying at the hotel there. Lord Kingsborough, his son, and John Hartney, a private in the militia, rode posthaste to Kilworth, unaware of the identity of the stranger, but suspicious of the worst. This was on Saturday, December 8.

What happened in the Kilworth hotel has been variously reported, but the reports agree that FitzGerald refused to open the door of his room, that the three men broke it in, and that Lord Kingsborough shot FitzGerald dead. Before he left the hotel for Moore Park, Lord K. had the presence of mind to search for and extract the threatening letter he had written FitzGerald. To Lady Mount Cashell he said immediately after the shooting,

"God! I don't know how I did it; but I most sincerely wish it had been by some other hand than mine."

Within a week, old Lord Kingston died at the age of seventy-two, Lord Kingsborough became the second Earl of Kingston, and Big George became Lord Kingsborough. When the charge of murder was brought against the three men present at the killing, Lord Kingston exercised his right to be tried, not by a jury, but by his peers in the Irish House of Lords. At the Cork assizes on April 9, 1798, a jury consisting of the first commoners of the county found Colonel King and John Hartney not guilty.

Friday, May 18, was the day appointed for the trial of Lord Kingston, and tickets, most difficult to come by, were issued for the house and galleries. The lords assembled at ten in the morning in their beautiful and commodious chamber—two marquesses, twenty-seven earls, fourteen viscounts, three archbishops, thirteen bishops, and fourteen barons. They then walked solemnly two-by-two in their robes of state from the House of Lords, which was too small to accommodate the throng, to the Colonnade in front of the building and thence to the House of Commons. This classic rotunda had galleries which would allow seven hundred spectators an uninterrupted view of the House. One portion of the chamber was covered with scarlet cloth and appropriated to the peeresses and their daughters, who ranged themselves in order of precedence. The commons, their families, and friends lined the galleries to witness the most majestic spectacle ever exhibited within those walls.

The Earl of Clare, bearing a white wand, presided as High Steward, the temporal peers (including Lord Mount Cashell) ranged on his left, the spiritual peers on his right, and the robed judges at a table in the center. Amidst reverences and ritual the proceedings went on: the reading of the King's commission, the writ of *certiorari*, and the indictment which said that Robert, Earl of Kingston, had discharged from a pistol a leaden bullet which had penetrated the left breast of Henry Gerard Fitz-Gerald to the depth of three inches, of which wound the said FitzGerald instantly died. Then came the moment that made the spectators shudder. The clerk of the crown directed the sergeant-at-arms to make proclamation: "Oyez, oyez, oyez. Constable of Dublin Castle, bring forth Robert Earl of Kingston, your prisoner, to the bar, pursuant to the order of the House of Lords. God save the King."

The Ulster King of Arms entered first, bearing the Kingston arms emblazoned on a shield. Next, amid dead silence, came Lord Kingston in black, moving with deliberate pace, his eyes fixed on the ground. Then came the executioner bearing an immense axe painted black to within two inches of the edge of bright and polished steel. He stood to the right of the prisoner and raised the axe, blade averted, to the height of Lord Kingston's neck. Should the verdict be guilty, the axe would be turned at once toward the condemned man, indicating his fate. Lord Kingston, after making low reverences to the High Steward and to the peers on either side of him, fell on his knees. The High Steward bade him rise and addressed him as follows:

"Robert Earl of Kingston, you are brought here to answer one of the most serious charges which can be made against any man,—a charge of the murder of a fellow subject. The solemnity and awful appearance of this judicature, must naturally discompose and embarrass your lordship. It may therefore not be improper in me to remind your lordship that you are to be tried by the laws of a free country, framed for the protection of innocence, and the punishment of guilt alone;—and it must be a great consolation to you to reflect, that you are to receive a trial before the supreme judicature of the nation, that you are to be tried by your peers, upon whose unbiased judgment and candour you may have the firmest reliance. . . ."

After the arraignment, the clerk of the crown said, "How say you Robert Earl of Kingston, are you guilty of this felony and murder in manner and form as you stand indicted and arraigned, or not?"

"Not guilty."

"Culprit, how will your lordship be tried?"

"By God and my peers."

"God send you a good deliverance."

A proclamation was then made for the witnesses for the prosecution to come forward, the widow of the deceased, his son Henry, and his daughter Caroline. Every eye was directed in anxious suspense toward the bar where the witnesses must appear, and every movement was interpreted as the appearance of some accuser. But none appeared, though Lord Kingston's counsel, J. P. Curran, testified that widow and children had been summoned.

The lords then retired to their own chamber, where the bishops begged to be exempted from voting. When they returned to the House of Commons, the High Steward called every peer by his name, beginning with the junior baron, and asked him, "Is Robert Earl of Kingston guilty of the felony and murder whereof he stands indicted?"

Every peer as he was called stood uncovered, his right hand upon his breast, and said, "Not guilty, upon my honor." This ceremony required an hour.

Lord Kingston was brought back to the bar, where he knelt until the High Steward bade him rise, saying,

"Robert Earl of Kingston, I have great satisfaction in informing you, that your peers upon whom you put yourself for trial, have without a dissenting voice, acquitted you of the crime whereof you stood indicted, and therefore you are discharged, paying your fees."

Lord Kingston made three reverences to the House and retired. The High Steward took his white wand in both hands, broke it in two, and declared the commission to be dissolved.

Lady Mary, with the resilience of youth, recovered from her ordeal. Seven years later she married a respectable gentleman, George Galbraith Meares of Meares Court, County Longford, and became the mother of four children. Her father, at forty-four, had less resilience. He died within a year and was buried at Mitchelstown in Kingston College Chapel.

CHAPTER 5.

ON THE MORNING of Friday, May 18, 1798, Lady Mount Cashell saw her father, a prisoner in black, stand beside the axe awaiting the verdict of his peers. The next evening, she was among the first to receive the news that Lord Edward FitzGerald, her friend and the military chief of the United Irishmen, had been captured and mortally wounded. To understand the import of that capture and that wound, it is necessary to review the political scene.

Grattan, in his *esto perpetua* speech proclaiming the achievement of the constitution of 1782, had said, "I am now addressing a free people." In point of fact he was not. The population of Ireland when he pronounced the words was roughly 4,500,000. Of these 450,000 were Protestants; 3,150,000 were Catholics; 900,000 were Dissenters. The "free people" he addressed were the Protestants, one-tenth of the population.

The masses, the Catholics, were separated from the Protestants by race, tradition, and language. They were not allowed to vote, to serve in Parliament, to hold office, to enter any profession save the medical, to indulge in trade, to own land, to possess a horse worth more than five pounds. They were excluded even from charities. In

Mitchelstown, miniature representative of the country, Kingston College was established for decayed gentry of the *Protestant* persuasion. The schools which Lady Kingsborough endowed for the poor on her estate were well attended at first, but, when she directed that the Sunday school be held in the Protestant church, the priest forbade Catholic children to attend. When the mistress of the weaving and spinning schools began the weaving and spinning with Protestant prayers, the Catholic children dropped out. Both sides were vexed; each side felt the other bigoted. Whoever was bigoted, the Catholic girls did not learn to spin and weave.[1]

The Dissenters, largely Presbyterian settlers in the North—puritan, republican, rational, industrious, dour—gratified their shocking need for hatred by dividing it among the Catholics and Protestant aristocrats. Thousands of them had emigrated to America and fought in the Revolution; the ones who remained were referred to by Lord Harcourt with some contempt as "the Presbyterians of the North who in their hearts are Americans." They suffered some of the legislative disabilities of the Catholics.

There remained the Protestants, one-tenth of the population served by a travesty of representation. Of the three hundred seats in the House of Commons, two hundred were private property. Bought votes and rotten pocket boroughs kept the reins in hands that had everything to lose and nothing to gain from slackening the grip. Who could expect a house of landlords to legislate land reform? The Lord Lieutenants, appointed by the King, received their instructions from England. When one of these, Lord Fitzwilliam, showed sympathetic inclination, he was recalled. Wolfe Tone summed it up: "The Revolution of 1782 was a Revolution which enabled Irishmen to sell at a much higher price their honor, their integrity, the interests of their country; it was a Revolution which, while at one stroke it doubled the value of every borough monger in the Kingdom, left three-fourths of our countrymen slaves as it found them."

Among the Protestants there were intellectuals like Wolfe Tone and Lady Mount Cashell who were influenced by the republican philosophy of France—and of Mary Wollstonecraft. They saw that religious differences were fostered by interested people who could derive nothing but profit from keeping Presbyterians and Catholics at each others' throats. The problem was to unite the two, to join logic with passion, to cause all Irishmen to face the modern world united by race rather than disunited by religion. This was the task of the United Irishmen.

The leadership was supplied by a witty, merry, gallant, civilized, free-thinking Protestant, Wolfe Tone. Tone was a Dubliner, a graduate of Trinity College, a lawyer, and a sympathizer with the French and American Revolutions. His simple plan was to unite the Presbyterians and Catholics, call in the aid of Republican France, and oust the English. At a meeting of thirteen men in Belfast on October 14, 1791, he founded the "Society of United Irishmen"; a few weeks later he created another branch in Dublin. Soon the sober reflections of republicanism were pulsating without sobriety in little groups of twelve throughout the land. Their object was "to make all Irishmen citizens and all citizens Irishmen." Their badge, overtly republican, consisted of a harp surmounted, not by a crown, but by a cap of liberty with the device IT IS NEW STRUNG AND SHALL BE HEARD.

The initiatory oath taken by all United Irishmen (after the society had been forced underground) reveals high purpose. "In the awful presence of God, I, ———, do voluntarily declare that I will persevere in endeavoring to form a brotherhood of affection among Irishmen of every *religious* persuasion, and that I will also persevere in my endeavors to obtain an equal, full, and adequate representation of *all* the people of Ireland. I do further declare, that neither hopes, fears, rewards, or punishments, shall ever induce me, directly or indirectly, to inform or give evidence against any member or members of this or similar societies, for any act or expression of theirs, done or made collectively or individually in or out of this society, in pursuance of the spirit of this obligation."

The military organization of the society, engrafted on the civil, was headed by Lord Edward FitzGerald, fifth son of the Duke of Leinster. After his education in France he was commissioned in the British Army. Lady Mount Cashell told Claire Clairmont the story that at eighteen he fought his first battle in the American Revolution. Complimented on his gallantry, he replied, "Ah! how much better I should have fought had I been on the other side."[2] After the war he explored Canadian forests, became adopted chief of a tribe of Hurons in Detroit, made his way down the Mississippi to New Orleans, and returned to Ireland to find that his brother had procured him a seat in the Irish Parliament. In 1792 when he went to Paris, where he lodged with Thomas Paine, he was predisposed to sympathize with the doctrines of republican France. He brought back to Ireland a French wife, Pamela (generally known as Lady Edward), as beautiful as he was handsome, and privy to his plans. It was inevitable that he would become a United Irishman.

The "army" that he commanded was, of course, poorly equipped; but he had, he believed, 280,000 men ready to rise at the signal. The men were generally between twenty and thirty years old, of sound physique and military disposition; they had able leaders; they needed only

to be properly armed—from France. What they did
have for arms were pikes, wooden shafts eight to twelve
feet long with iron heads sometimes hooked at the side.
Useless weapons for fighting at any distance, pikes were
effective in close combat, and no cavalry could withstand
them. One prod from a pike would cause a horse to rear,
either throwing the rider or making it impossible for him
to use his sword. All over Ireland blacksmiths were forging pike heads. Young men were paying one-and-six to
join the United Irishmen and get a pike.

What precise part Lady Mount Cashell played in the
movement is not known; we do know that she was a
republican, called herself a United Irishwoman,[3] and was
under suspicion of the government.[4] Perhaps she was prepared to be a heroine. Certainly the distance between herself and Lord Mount Cashell was widened.

2

The antithesis of Lady Mount Cashell's every thought
and feeling on the subject of patriotism was exemplified
by her brother George, Lord Kingsborough. He was an
Orangeman. The first Orange Lodge, composed of royal-
ists dedicated to the continuance of the Protestant Ascend-
ancy, was founded in 1795 to counteract the work of the
United Irishmen. The Orange oath, as frequently published, has the sound of a rebound from that of the
United Irishmen. "I, ——, do swear, that I will be
true to King and Government; and that I will exterminate
the Catholics of Ireland, as far as in my power lies."
(The extermination clause has been vehemently denied by
Orangemen, who ought to know.)

Sir Jonah Barrington, a charter member, has given
the full Orange toast with a spirited description of its
ritual on the favorite night of assembly, the first of July,

the anniversary of the Battle of the Boyne, when William
of Orange defeated the Irish Jacobites. Every man in
Sir Jonah's lodge unbuttoned the knees of his breeches
and "with extraordinary zeal" drank the toast on his bare
joints:

TO

The glorious—pious—and immortal memory of the
great and good King William: not forgetting Oliver
Cromwell, who assisted in redeeming us from popery,
slavery, arbitrary power, brass-money, and wooden shoes.
May we never want a Williamite to kick the ***** [his
asterisks] of a Jacobite! and a ***** for the bishop of
Cork! And he that won't drink this, whether he be
priest, bishop, deacon, bellows-blower, grave-digger, or
any other of the fraternity *of the clergy;* may a north
wind blow him to the south, and a west wind blow him to
the east! May he have a dark night—a lee shore, a rank
storm, and a leaky vessel, to carry him over the river
Styx! May the dog Cerberus make a meal of his r—p,
and Pluto, a snuff-box of his skull; and may the devil
jump down his throat with a red-hot harrow, with every
pin tear out a gut, and blow him with a clean carcass to
hell! *Amen.*[5]

The members then rose from their knees, rebuttoned their
breeches, and proceeded to what Sir Jonah calls their
serious work, the consumption of whiskey, rum, and porter
in testimony of their loyalty to king and faith.

If the Orange Lodges may be said to have had a military wing, such was to be found in the militia and the yeomanry. The government could count on 15,000 regular
Hessian and English troops, 18,000 militia, and 50,000
yeomen. The militia were officered by Protestants, frequently Orangemen, with Catholics among the rank and

file; the yeomen were Irish Protestant tenants and townsmen commanded by commissioned gentry. The soldiery
lived at free quarters on the people.

Lord Kingsborough, Big George, was Colonel and
Commander of the North Cork Regiment of Militia (No.
34), consisting of 26 officers, 24 sergeants, 16 drummers,
12 fifers, and 546 rank and file. A full century after his
death the name "North Cork" could still put terror into
the hearts of Wexford peasants. There is a Mitchelstown
story concerning Lord Kingsborough, one John O'Mahony, and his Protestant friend Raymond Philip, son of
a lieutenant in the Mounted Yeomanry. One evening
O'Mahony was paying a call on young Philip when the
clatter of horses' hoofs warned them that the Orangemen
were riding. Philip hid O'Mahony in the wall near his
fireplace, placing a chair in front of the door to the recess.
Booted and spurred, Big George entered, sat in the maneuvered chair, and announced that he was looking for
O'Mahony, who had returned to Ireland after communi-
cating with the French Directory. Furthermore, arms
had been stolen the night before from Orange Lodge.
"If I can catch him I will hang him on the nearest tree,"
vowed George, ordering Philip to serve whiskey to the
men outside. Inside the recess, O'Mahony loosened his
two pistols, determined to sell his life for Lord Kingsborough's. It wasn't necessary: after drinking the whiskey, Big George and his men rode off into the night to
burn down a Catholic chapel near Ballyporeen.[6]

Such an outrage was not unique. The army was
shockingly out of hand, "in such a state of licentiousness,"
reported their English general, "as must render it formid-
able to every one but the enemy." Floggings, burnings,
tortures, shootings, hangings were the order of the day.
Even the most innocent man, woman, or child was liable

to savagery: anyone under suspicion was eligible. A youth named Bergan, for example, was flogged to death for possessing a ring with the device of the shamrock. There was truth in the lines

'Tis the most distressful country that ever I have seen,
They're hanging men and women for the wearing of
    the green.

The yeomanry pursued their excesses to such an extent that one may conclude that torture was for them a sport. The Protestant officers of the militia imprudently flaunted their prejudices before the Catholic rank and file. Their real purpose may well have been not to put down rebellion but to provoke it, not to train the militia but to encourage desertion.

Big George is credited with one refinement on the methods of torture—the pitchcap. A cap of paper or linen containing melted pitch was placed on the head of the victim, who was then set loose to run maddened through the streets followed by his tormentors, officers, and gentlemen. Sometimes the cap was turpentined and set on fire; sometimes it was torn from the head bringing with it hair and skin. It was one of the most effective methods of extracting information from suspects, even from people who had nothing to tell.

3

When the plans of the United Irishmen were articulated in every detail, the night of May 23, 1798, was selected for the general rising. Wolfe Tone was in Paris, trying with desperation to raise a French expedition. The leaders in Ireland were in hiding. On the eve, the government struck; the Society had been honeycombed with treachery after all; the leaders were arrested. Shorn of their leaders, the people lost heart; there almost was no rebellion.

Lord Edward FitzGerald had been underground for some time, spending no more than two or three nights under one roof, awaiting the day when he could don the uniform of commander. Twice in disguise he visited his wife at Moira House; sometimes he had six or seven people in to dinner; in general he observed less caution than his situation required. With a price of £1,000 on his head, it is surprising that he avoided apprehension as long as he did. On May 17, Ascension Thursday, while going through the streets with an armed party, he was attacked, but escaped. "Of the precise object or destination of this party," wrote his biographer, Thomas Moore, "I have not been able to make out any thing certain; but if, as is generally supposed, Lord Edward was at the time on his way to Moira-house. . . ."[7] In her copy of the biography Lady Mount Cashell wrote beside this passage the words "not true"; she was, it appears, better acquainted with Lord Edward's movements than was his biographer.

At nine o'clock on Saturday night, Lord Edward was taken and wounded in a house on Thomas Street. Lady Mount Cashell at once dispatched a servant to forbid Lady Edward's servants saying anything to Lady Edward that night. Perhaps he might yet be rescued; but the news was still bad on Sunday morning, when Lady Edward had to be told. She bore it better than her friends had expected.

Our story now becomes the story of the North Cork Militia,[8] commanded by Lady Mount Cashell's brother and officered by her neighbors in County Cork, neighbors who had been her dinner guests at Moore Park, gentry with sympathies opposed to the sympathies of the United Irishmen she entertained in Dublin. It would be agreeable to report that the North Cork distinguished itself for any virtue—humanity, courage, gallantry, or strategy—in service of the King.

On Wednesday, May 23, the evening of the scheduled uprising, drums beat to arms within earshot of Mount Cashell House, and the North Cork assembled on St. Stephen's Green in Dublin to the number of 432. The troops had been hurried into the city and quartered in the George's Street Barracks to protect the government and capital against the rebels. Big George saw that his men were ready, but they were not needed: the proposed attack on Dublin Castle and release of the prisoners in Newgate Jail never really came off.

On Thursday, May 24, a detachment of North Cork men at Prosperous in County Kildare, seventeen miles from Dublin, was slaughtered. On the previous Sunday, Captain Swayne had arrived with forty North Cork men, had attended the Catholic chapel with Dr. Esmond, a wealthy Protestant of local influence, and had asked the people to give up their arms. The appeal proving ineffective, Captain Swayne was obliged to resort to some coercive measures: seizure of cattle, burnings, floggings, and other ingenuities which had produced results in County Cork. Dr. Esmond then transmitted the news that the people were afraid to comply, but that they were prepared to deposit their arms in the streets under cover of darkness, if allowed to enter the town unchallenged. This seemed reasonable to Captain Swayne, who dined with Dr. Esmond, enjoying the "glow of mirth" until midnight. At two in the morning the victims of the coercive measures entered the town unchallenged and unmolested, killed the two sentries, and set fire to the barracks. The suffocating soldiers mounted to the second floor. Overcome by heat, smoke, and flames, in despair they leaped from the windows of the flaming building to be impaled below on expectant pikes. None escaped.

On Friday, May 25, a company of the North Cork was engaged, with regulars and yeomanry, in the defense of the town of Carlow. A garrison of five hundred armed troops routed some fifteen hundred pikemen. That evening and all the next day nineteen carts were employed in carrying dead rebels from the streets to gravel pits where the bodies were buried and covered with quicklime. After the defeat, the soldiers executed about two hundred prisoners.

On Whitsunday, May 27, Colonel Foote marched with a detachment of 110 men of the North Cork to Oulart Hill, eight miles from the town of Wexford, where Father John Murphy headed some four thousand rebels. When the rebels retreated up the hill, the exultant militia rushed forward crying that they would beat them out of the field. Then the pikemen turned on their pursuers; of the 110 North Cork men who had set out at eleven in the morning, only Colonel Foote, a sergeant, and three privates returned.

On May 28, Father Murphy led his men, whose numbers were swelling by the thousands, to the town of Enniscorthy, twelve miles from Wexford. The town was defended by some two hundred local yeomanry and one hundred men of the North Cork under Captain Snowe and Lieutenant Bowen. The yeomanry took up their position outside the gate; North Cork defended the bridge. After three hours of fighting, Captain Snowe evacuated the burning town.

On May 30, the North Cork behaved badly. Three hundred of their militia were at stations guarding the entrances to the town of Wexford. As the rebels approached, all the officers except one lad of fourteen deserted the troops and boarded ships in Wexford harbor. When the rebels arrived, the unofficered troops fled in great disorder. Fifty of them were taken prisoner. The town of Wexford fell.

On June 5 at New Ross, fourteen hundred government troops, North Cork among them, met over twenty thousand rebels. A sergeant of the regulars with two ship guns and sixteen men cut lanes in the ranks of the pikemen. One computation of the rebel dead reads: "Three thousand four hundred buried. Sixty-two cart-loads thrown into the river. Sixty cart-loads taken away by the rebels." Why continue? The story is the same. It is a story of North Cork stupidity and cowardice in the face of danger; of ferocity and outrage in the wake of victory.

But what of Big George? He was not needed in Dublin, for the real insurrection had taken place, surprisingly, in Wexford, where the United Irishmen had not been organized. George left Dublin with two of his officers to join his regiment and entered Wexford harbor in a hired boat not knowing that the town had fallen. Captured before he could put ashore, his life was in danger, for many of the rebels would have liked nothing better than to use the pitch cap on him, especially after one was found in the barracks. An angry mob, with the pitch cap raised aloft on a pike like a standard, surrounded The Cape of Good Hope, the inn where Big George was held prisoner. But sailors defended him against the mob, for their leaders thought that he would be a valuable hostage, useful in making terms with the government should it be necessary.

It was necessary. On June 21, when it became apparent that the town would be taken by thousands of government reinforcements, it was decided that Lord Kingsborough should inform the commanders of the

King's forces that the town had surrendered to him and
that he had "pledged his honor in the most solemn manner" that the persons and property of the townspeople
would be protected. Big George was liberated and sent
to General Sir John Moore with the message. The
King's troops entered the town unopposed, put all the
wounded to the sword, and killed off the stragglers that
they encountered.

At Windsor, Her Majesty Queen Charlotte drove up
in her carriage to Lady Kingston's cottage. "I have
ventured to call upon your ladyship," said the Queen,
"to tell you that Lord Kingsborough is safe. I think the
news we have had at the castle may be earlier than what
your ladyship may have received."[9]

After the rebellion was suppressed, the militia and
yeomanry played the role of the avenging angel. Pillage,
murder, burning, flogging continued to provoke feeble
retaliation on the part of the rebels. "I am convinced,"
General Moore reported officially, "the country would
again be quiet if the gentlemen and yeomen could behave
themselves with tolerable decency and prudence. . . . I
cannot but think that it was their harshness and ill-treat-
ment that in a great measure drove the peasants and
farmers to revolt." Lord Cornwallis in the double office
of Lord Lieutenant and Commander-in-Chief used all of
his great abilities and good will to restore order. He reported that the militia was as contemptible in the face of
any serious resistance as it was ferocious in its treatment
of unarmed wretches. Most commentators single out the
North Cork Regiment of Militia as having been especially
barbarous.

Lady Mount Cashell lived through all this—the capture and death of Lord Edward, the call to arms, the
failure of her republican principles, the reign of terror.

The rebellion was just about over when she gave birth to her fourth child, Edward George, on August 18.

4

The rebellion was, in the last analysis, not conducted on its initial principles of liberty, equality, and fraternity. Rather it had been a revolt of peasants and farmers goaded into furious retaliation. Cowed, beaten, crushed, and disillusioned, the country settled into a deadly lull, held in subjection by a hundred thousand troops. Now was the time for William Pitt and the ruling junta to effect their long-felt desire, a legislative union with Great Britain by which the Irish Parliament was to be dissolved, and Ireland to be represented by 100 out of 660 members in the British House of Commons and by 32 peers in the House of Lords. On any vote on any issue the Irish could be swamped. Grattan's Parliament had made Ireland prosperous; the Union was to turn Ireland into a squalid shire.

In 1799 the British House of Commons voted in favor of the Union; the Irish House defeated the bill. Pitt and the junta had to buy out the Irish Parliament. Twenty-eight members of Parliament were elevated to the peerage in return for their votes; twenty additional lords were advanced. The pocket boroughs were bought for £1,260,000 (chargeable to Ireland). Pensions, sinecures, jobs in the army, navy, and diplomatic service were promised to members and their relatives. Men who accepted £8,000 for their votes spent the remainder of their lives in regret that they had not been as astute as their colleagues who had received the sum down *and* a pension. Against the wish of the country, against protests from every source, the Irish House of Commons

voted for the Union in June of 1800. On August 1, King
George III gave royal assent.

Of course, the House of Lords went with the junta;
but there was a protest from twenty of the peers. "We
cannot help observing," they protested, "that the terms
proposed in the said Bill are inconsistent with those
principles [recommended by our most gracious sovereign],
and are totally unequal; that Great Britain is thereby
to retain entire and undiminished her Houses of Lords
and Commons, and that two-fifteenths of the Irish peers
are to be degraded and deprived of their legislative func-
tions, and that two-thirds of the Irish House of Commons
are to be struck off. . . .

"We have endeavoured to interpose our votes, and
failing, we transmit to after-times our names in solemn
protest on behalf of the parliamentary constitution of
this realm, the liberty which it secured, the trade which it
protected, the connection which it preserved, and the constitution which it supplied and fortified. This we feel
ourselves called upon to do in support of our characters,
our honour, and whatever is left us worthy to be transmitted to our posterity." The name of Lord Mount
Cashell is among the names of the twenty Irish Lords
protesting.[10]

With the legislature gone, Dublin changed from the
seventh city of Christendom to a dull, stagnating, pro-
vincial city without grace or luster. The fashionables followed Parliament across the channel; there was no need
for noblemen's seats in the capital; absentees continued to
collect their rents which they spent abroad. One need but
contrast the silverware, medallions, dinner service, chimney pieces, the type and binding of books that Ireland
produced before the Union with the nothing that came
after to appreciate what happened.

Henrietta Street, one of the finest residential streets in Europe, lined with the mansions of noblemen and primates, began its descent to the ultimate slum. Mantels, doors, stairways were bought at bargain prices and sent to England. The parlor which Mary Wollstonecraft had to entertain her male visitors came to accommodate a slum family. The steps which the Countess of Westmorland had mounted to attend Lady Kingsborough's rout, a £500 dress on her back, became a playground for skinny-limbed, lank-haired, dirty-faced, stone-throwing urchins. The panes of glass in the delicate fanlight were broken and never replaced. The history of the house emerges as the symbolic history of the Ireland of its time. Early in our own century, a wealthy English lady instructed her agent to purchase Henrietta Street for her and to restore the Georgian buildings. Her agent discontinued negotiations when he discovered that the acrid odor of the slums had impregnated the woodwork and could not be removed.[11]

The two Irish lords proudly responsible for the Union were the Earl of Clare and Viscount Castlereagh. When Lord Clare died, a year after the Union had been effected, the people threw dead cats on his coffin. Lord Castlereagh moved to London, where he enjoyed a position of great power and eminence in the English government until he cut his throat with a penknife in 1822. The Act of Union was a greater blow to Lady Mount Cashell and her liberal principles than even the Rebellion of '98. Twenty years after the Union she said that her nerves had not then recovered from the shock.[12]

CHAPTER 6.

WHEN Lady Mount Cashell wrote to Godwin on August 6, 1801, she was busy with a number of details, for the Mount Cashells were planning a three-months' excursion to England. Within a month their plans had been enlarged to include a trip to the Continent, now that the wars were over and traveling was again practicable in the French Republic. Miss Catherine Wilmot, who had been introduced to Lady M. by the Bishop of Ripon,[1] had recently received a legacy from her grandmother, and she, too, was eager to go abroad. Miss Wilmot, a spirited Irish gentlewoman of twenty-eight—a year younger than Lady M.—kept a journal for the next two years in the form of letters she wrote from the Continent to her brother back home.

The party that left Ireland in September included Lord and Lady Mount Cashell, their two daughters Helena and Jane, Miss Wilmot, and four servants. The boys—Stephen, Robert, and Edward—were left in the charge of their tutor, Mr. Egan, and were to join their parents later in Paris. For two months the party stayed in London at 54 St. James' Street, meeting so many remarkable people that Miss Wilmot regretted not having begun her journal then. Among these remarkable people was William Godwin, whose diary records the exchange of half a dozen calls between September 29 and November 21.[2] Once he met the ladies by accident at the theater.

Mary Wollstonecraft had been dead four years, and Godwin had been proposing to sundry women, not only because he wanted a wife, but also because he wanted a mother for Mary's two children, Fanny Imlay and Mary Godwin. He had been unsuccessfully aggressive in his proposals, though not so aggressive as the woman he finally won. Mrs. Mary Jane Clairmont, a buxom widow of thirty-five with two children, Charles and Mary Jane, lived next door. In May she had precipitated their meeting when she leaned out of her balcony window and cried, "Is it possible that I behold the immortal Godwin?" In December they were married. But he was still single and courting when Lady Mount Cashell and Miss Wilmot called. He gave them letters of introduction to two of his radical friends in Paris, one of whom was Thomas Holcroft.

On November 24 they departed from London, the Mount Cashells and Miss Wilmot in the family coach, the four servants—Mary Lawless, Mary Smith, Blanchois, and William—in a second carriage, "nine Irish Adventurers," said Miss Wilmot, "driving full speed." At three in the morning of the twenty-ninth, travelers and carriages boarded the *Countess of Elgin* at Dover, in Lady Mount Cashell's suite a smuggled young Frenchman who could not get a passport. After a five-hour crossing, they were in France. Reading Miss Wilmot's journal is a delight, because she was an enthusiastic and intelligent woman who saw everything with fresh eyes and, like many novice travelers, fell in love with everything she saw.

The customs officers in Republican France were thorough to a fault. After combing the luggage, they put their hands into the travelers' pockets and felt down their sides as far as the ankles searching for contraband. Somehow, they did not seem to notice the smuggled Frenchman. Miss Wilmot found everything different and worth journalizing: cocked hats, tricolor cockades, men with gold earrings and muffs, wooden shoes, magnificent meals, republican tunes played outside their windows at Dessein's Hotel, a hundred compliments paid to "Mi Lor Anglais." The republicans were not unimpressed by the coat-of-arms on the family coach.

At Abbeville the smuggled Frenchman joined his family, who, warned in advance, had invited all the country to a grand ball in honor of the liberators. At their little inn at Cormont they were served as large a dish of potatoes as they could have got in Ireland. At Amiens Lord M. paid a call on Lord Cornwallis, there for the treaty of peace, while the ladies "trotted off" to see the Cathedral. On December 5 at four o'clock they drove into Paris, their "eyes flying out of their sockets," and lodged at the Hôtel de l'Europe. Like travelers before them and travelers after them, they discovered in Paris a system of extortion. Lord M. had recourse to the Commissary, and justice was allotted, but the Mount Cashells removed anyway to the Hôtel d'Espagne at eighteen *louis d'ors* the month.

Immediately upon her arrival in Paris, Lady Mount Cashell sent off Godwin's letter of introduction to Thomas Holcroft, who, with some alacrity, called on her in the Hôtel d'Espagne and became a constant visitor. She was predisposed to like this dramatist son of a shoemaker for many reasons: Godwin had introduced him, his conversation was rational and moral, he had been indicted for high treason. Although she herself was "too apt to form favourable opinions precipitately," her husband and her companion did not suffer under such a burden. Lord M. took a complete dislike to the man, and Miss Wilmot wrote in her journal, "I feel as if I should like to say a hundred bitter things" about him.

But Lady Mount Cashell esteemed him enough to ask him to recommend a governess for her daughters. Holcroft knew of only one qualified person in Paris, who, as luck would have it, was his daughter Fanny, a well-educated and highly accomplished young lady, it appeared. Fanny was persuaded. Soon, to all the household, there became apparent a discrepancy between appearance and reality. "Luckless" Fanny could not take anything into her hands but she would let it fall. She paid no heed to the children, for they tended to interfere with her writing of poetry. Lady Mount Cashell, with some good humor, later described Fanny to Claire Clairmont, who put the description into her journal.

"Did a great man enter the house she wrote Poetry—a little one?—she wrote poetry—was there a party to dinner she wrote poetry. Was there no party to dinner? Still she wrote poetry—and such poetry! She was called down by one of the servants on the arrival of a party of strangers. She rushed into the room, breathless and with a pen in her hand. 'Ah! my God!' said she! 'have the kindness to excuse me. I have left my heroine in my hero's arms and I must fly to relieve them'—so saying she disappeared to the great astonishment of all the company."[3]

But this was not the worst. One morning she was found missing. She was sought for and pursued; when recovered, she explained that she had run off with a gentleman, but the only identification of the gentleman that she could give was that he wore a green coat. In spite of her clumsy goodness of heart, her music, and her knowledge of modern languages, she was a most unfit person to be entrusted with the education of two little girls.

Within three weeks Lady Mount Cashell thought she had found a civilized means of dismissing Fanny without hurting the feelings of either father or daughter. Some officious persons had informed Lord Mount Cashell that Holcroft had been tried for high treason, that he and other acquaintances in Paris were notorious English democrats, and that it would be well for loyal British subjects to avoid him. She invited Holcroft to one of her "public nights," where she showed him every civility, placing Fanny at the pianoforte to play and sing and tendering every compliment to the young lady's accomplishments. When Holcroft left, Lady M. placed in his hands a letter to the effect that Lord M. had been warned of Holcroft's political history and that domestic peace required her to part with Fanny. Holcroft flew into a rage and made preparations to publish the whole thing to the world, showing how a Peeress could behave to a Poet and how an innocent daughter could be persecuted for the opinions of her father. Lady M. called on Holcroft to forestall obtruding a private transaction on the public eye, only to find that her rational and moral friend was violent beyond the power of cool discussion. When he insisted on publishing his story, she had the odious task of presenting him with all the causes of his daughter's dismissal. Her additional causes were that Fanny had "an uncultivation of understanding, a want of polish of mind, and an entire absence of those numerous little delicacies easier to be imagined than expressed."

An implacable Holcroft sent his version to Godwin to be published; but Lady Mount Cashell sent hers as well, with confirmation from a "rational friend." The story was not discovered to the world. Nor was the gentleman in the green coat.[4]

Of course, the ladies indulged every desire to see the sights of Paris. They saw museums recently enriched by Napoleon's plunder of Italy with Venuses of this and Apollos of that. (General de Grouchy said, looking across the table at Lady Mount Cashell, that it was not necessary to go to Italy to find Venuses.) They saw churches transformed from the glory of God to the glory of Man, into stables, storehouses, or magazines. They went to the opera, at which decorum was such that not a whisper was to be heard. (Once Miss Wilmot inadvertently draped her shawl over the side of her box, and a gentleman whispered to her that she must draw it back lest a tumult ensue and the performance be suspended.)

When the first French women called on the Mount Cashells, they thought that some of the statues in the Louvre had come to life and stepped off their pedestals to return their morning call. Madame Rose and her three daughters glided into the rooms like Greek goddesses. Daughter Victoire was dressed like Diana in a sleeveless gown of almost transparent drapery, a gold chain wound around the upper part of her arm, her neck exposed, and her hair arranged in a crescent. They kissed the Irish ladies on both cheeks and showed so much ease, affection, and animation that Lady Mount Cashell exclaimed, "Lord bless me, how pleasant French manners are!"[5] At their first *Thé*, the Irish ladies were astounded to see women from seventeen to seventy "almost in a state of nature," with trains half the length of the room. When Madame de Soubiran gave her ball for all nations, she was undressed in the latest Parisian fashion, with a cameo of Jupiter attached to her shawl, Solon hanging from one ear,

Pericles from the other, Socrates attached to her zone, Xenophon and Plato on either arm. "There was so much rouge on the cheeks of all the ladies," Miss Wilmot said, "that handsome as Lady Mount Cashell is, her face look'd pale and cold, like a frosty moon. . . ."[6] Little girls frequently dressed as boys, but when they did wear petticoats they were miniatures of their mothers, with gracefully managed trains and their hair *à la grecque*. It was quite the fashion for women to be good mothers, many of whom nursed their own children. It was also the fashion for husbands and wives to appear to love each other in public, even though they might be negotiating a divorce in private.

Miss Wilmot was surprised not to find a spark of republicanism among the French whom she met. They were full of nostalgia for the past and fond of rank, honors, and every etiquette that distinguished them from the rabble. The lower orders, though, made a great show of independence. Napoleon's effigy was everywhere—on ladies' reticules, on every gingerbread stall, even on pieces of barley sugar one swallowed to cure a cold.

Early in January the Mount Cashells moved to the Hôtel de Rome, which before the Revolution had been the home of the Duchesse de La Vallière, Louis XIV's mistress. There for twenty-five *louis d'ors* a month they rented magnificent apartments consisting of antechamber, drawing room, dining room, bedrooms for the Mount Cashells, Miss Wilmot, the children, and the servants, and balconies overlooking the gardens and the Temple of Mars. From these headquarters on the Faubourg St. Germain they went forth to breakfasts and dinners and teas and plays and balls and soirées and assemblies and masquerades. And here they gave their own receptions to fifty, or seventy, or a hundred people.

Among the English with whom they associated were Francis James Jackson, the Plenipotentiary to France; General Sir Henry Pigot, to whom Malta surrendered; Cardinal Erskine, who walked in the hotel gardens with the ladies; Lord Henry Petty, who became third Marquess of Lansdowne; the Right Honorable Charles James Fox; John Philip Kemble, the actor; Helen Maria Williams, who conducted a liberal salon; John Hurford Stone, who befriended Charlotte Corday at her trial; and Thomas Paine, who imagined that every woman he met fell in love with him.

Among the Irish were Lord Cahir and Lady Cahir, of Blarney Castle; Lady Crofton; William and Sophia, son and daughter of Sir John Parnell; Lord Concurry and his two sisters; Richard Trench, father of the Archbishop of Dublin; St. George Caulfield; the St. Legers; James Penrose of Woodhill, County Cork; the widow of Wolfe Tone, who had killed himself in prison awaiting hanging in '98; and Robert Emmet, the darling of Erin, who was to be hanged within two years. (Lady Mount Cashell was appealed to for help in finding a French school for Wolfe Tone's boys.)

Among the Americans were Sir Benjamin Thompson, of Rumford, New Hampshire, who had raised a regiment for George III and who had been created Count Rumford by the Elector of Bavaria; William Loughton Smith, the Ambassador to Portugal; Robert R. Livingston, the Minister to France who negotiated the Louisiana Purchase; Charles Pinckney Horry, of South Carolina, who married a niece of Lafayette's; and Joel Barlow, whose revolutionary writings made him more welcome in Paris than in London.

Among the French were Madame de Soubiran and Madame Karagnan and Madame de la Croix and Madame

de Viot, Parisian *beaux esprits;* M. le Général de Château
Neuf, who prided himself on being the illegitimate son of
Louis XVI; M. Pougence, the illegitimate son of the
Prince de Condé; General Alexandre Berthier and General
Moreau and General Masséna and General MacDonald
and General de Grouchy, who was second in command at
Bantry Bay; the Abbé Sieyès and the Abbé Sicard and the
Bishop of Blois, who had defied the Reign of Terror; Jo-
seph de la Lande, the astronomer; Jean Chaptal, the
chemist; Joseph Montgolfier, inventor of the balloon;
Jacques Louis David, Napoleon's court painter; Jean
François de la Harpe, who educated the Emperor of Rus-
sia; Lazare Carnot, who created the fourteen armies of the
Republic; the Marquis de Lafayette, who had helped the
Americans; Talleyrand, who gobbled his food like a duck;
Madame Bonaparte, to whom the Irish ladies were pre-
sented; and Bonaparte himself, who had them in to dine.
(Lady Mount Cashell, looking beautiful in black crêpe
and diamonds, was handed in to dinner by the English
Minister.)

Also there were the Swedish Ambassador and Madame
de Staël-Holstein; Ali Effendi, the Ottoman Ambassador,
who was thrown into a rage when some heretical drops of
champagne sprinkled his ermined sleeve; Lucasina, the
Prussian Ambassador; Baron d'Armfelt, the Finn; Cardinal Caprara, the Pope's legate who concluded the Con-
cordat with Napoleon; the Princess di Belmonte, an
Italian of seventy who traveled always with her *cicisbeo;*
Count and Countess Myscelska, who served Lady Mount
Cashell a meal consisting of potatoes cooked in fifty different ways; Russian princes and princesses without number; and General Kosciusko, who played games on the
floor with the Mount Cashell children.

In June the party was increased by five upon the

arrival of the three elder boys with their tutor, Mr. Egan, and Mrs. Ruaud, governess to the girls. The family was further augmented in July by another son, who, according to law, was two days later presented to the municipality and inscribed in the archives as a new *citoyen*. When he was christened Richard Francis Stanislas, there was great "junketing," according to Miss Wilmot. The godparents were Mr. William Parnell, the Polish Countess Myscelska, and Mr. Livingston, the American Minister. The Countess Myscelska had the good fortune to possess enough rank and wealth to allow her to be completely unaffected in her manners. She asked Lady Mount Cashell for the gift of a tree, for in Poland the countess had a plantation consisting of trees given to her by friends, the trees appropriately suggesting the friends as the countess walked among them. Lady Mount Cashell presented her with an arbutus as being common in Ireland.

Once while Lord Mount Cashell was away on an expedition to Orléans, the two ladies indulged one of their whims. Like Cleopatra before them, they went slumming on the boulevards, in the cabarets and cafés, "poking our noses into every haunt of the lower order of people" —accompanied by two or three gentlemen, it should be said. Sometimes they would pay two sous to attend one of the theaters, delighted with what they saw, and finding even in the meanest places "Elegant Decorum."

After having spent more than nine months in Paris, the Mount Cashells reluctantly departed in order to spend the winter in Italy, cheered by the prospect of returning to Paris on their way back to Ireland. On Wednesday, September 15, the governess and the two girls, the tutor with Robert and Edward, and Mary Lawless, the children's maid, set off in the family coach, William the groom riding courier. The next day the remainder of the party took leave: Lady M., the infant, and Mary Smith in the chaise, with Lord Mount Cashell, Lord Kilworth, and Miss Wilmot in a newly purchased French carriage. A new member of the group, Para, rode as *avant courier*, dressed in a gold-trimmed blue jacket, nightcap, and holsters.

Their first stop was at Fontainebleau where they visited the château, took the baths, and listened to a story that Sophé, the innkeeper's daughter, told them about an old, white-bearded hermit who had lived in a cave in the forest for thirty-six years to expiate some sin of his youth. On Saturday they rode fifty-four miles to Briare, and on Sunday fifty-two miles to Nevers. At Lyons Lord Mount Cashell hired a flat-bottomed boat large enough to take on the three carriages, fifteen people, and three gentlemen from Lyons, in addition to the crew. In this agreeable manner they sailed down the Rhône for five days and sixty leagues until they reached Avignon. There they said good-by to their sailors, and continued on the road to Nîmes.

They remained a week in Nîmes, where Lord M. purchased a house for the children, their tutor, and governess to occupy while Lord and Lady M., Miss Wilmot, and little Richard spent the winter in Italy.

Travelers who have taken the train from France to Italy through the Mt. Cenis tunnel will be interested to know how the Mount Cashells crossed the mountain one hundred and fifty years ago. For four days they traveled in their carriages from Nîmes to Montmeyan in Savoy. Then they spent thirteen hours a day for three days passing through rocky valleys until they were ready to begin the ascent of the mountain, which Miss Wilmot thought to be three miles high. At this point they were tied on litters, muzzled, and packed in straw, while twenty or thirty wild-spirited Savoyards undertook to carry them across the mountains. While one crew carried the litters, the remaining Savoyards ran alongside or full-speed ahead, singing, leaping from rock to rock, and in general showing off. Whenever they approached a little mountain village, they set up a wild song which brought out all the villagers to welcome the travelers, while the Savoyards regaled themselves with the *vin du pays* and the travelers fed on mountain trout.

At Turin they stayed for two weeks seeing the sights, being entertained by the people to whom Lady Mount Cashell had letters, and envying their own servants the opportunity of mingling with the people and becoming acquainted with the customs of the country. After ten days in Milan and "loitering" in Pavia, Piacenza, Parma, Modena, and Bologna, they arrived in Florence on November 27. A few miles out of Pavia, a torrential rain forced them to spend the night in a haunted-looking house in the midst of the country of the banditti. The room they were given was in monstrous disorder, the knife-slashed table overturned, a picture of Jesus hanging upside down, and warnings scrawled with blood and charcoal on the walls. Some surly men threw mattresses of straw on the floor and reluctantly brought wood for the fire. Lady M. and Miss Wilmot lay awake listening to the rain and wind and the voices of men in the room below them. Sometimes Para's voice would precede a violent burst of laughter. Surprisingly, the terrified ladies dozed off to be awakened by Para's unlocking the door in the morning. He, William, and the two *voituriers*, armed with pistols and stilettos, had sat up all night drinking and joking with the sinister-looking men of the inn. Para, in his experience, was convinced that they had spent the night in the very worst den of assassins.

They remained only three weeks in Florence. Monsignore Morozzo, the Pope's Nuncio, called the first evening. Then the Princess Montemiletto and the Minister of the Italian Republic came to take them to the theater. They fell in love with the princess, an educated, sensible, and unpretentious Neapolitan who had taken political refuge in Florence. The next evening the Marchese Santini came to take them to visit the Countess of Albany, widow of Prince Charles Edward Stuart. They were not impressed by the social graces of her lover, Count Alfieri, even though he was called the "Shakespeare of Italy." Signora Bellini gave an enchanting harp concert, accompanied on the harpsicord by her *cicisbeo;* and the Marchese Torrigiani gave two elegant balls at which Prince Corsini danced with Miss Wilmot.

The Irish ladies were somewhat shocked by Italian customs. Husbands and wives, however much they loved each other, were never seen together outside their own homes. In public, ladies were attended by a *cavalier servente,* who functioned as lover, guardian, or servant. Ladies of the highest rank would have several of these: first the favorite or *cicisbeo,* then the *ganzo,* then the *aspirante,* and finally the *patico,* numbers two, three, and four aspiring to rise when one, two, and three were cashiered. Shortly before the arrival of the Mount Cashells, La Bentivoglia, "a sad virago of a woman," had thrashed the Prince Corsini, her *cavalier servente,* within an inch of his life. But the prince and La Bentivoglia had patched things up.

After three weeks in Florence the Mount Cashells departed for Naples, planning to return to Florence in April. The trip to Naples occupied thirteen days, including stops in Siena for the cathedral, in Montefiascone for the wine, and in Rome for the Christmas ceremonies.

They did not have the opportunity to become well acquainted with St. Peter's, because there were so many English present that the Mount Cashells did nothing but give and receive greetings during all the time they were there. On New Year's Day of 1803 they rode into the brave new world of Naples.

Again it is refreshing to look at the sights through the wide eyes of Miss Wilmot: little carriages like China flowerpots, magnificent equipages in gay procession, beflowered and beribboned horses, lazzaroni eating macaroni, monks singing dirges, *improvvisatori* haranguing mobs, painted barks by the thousands in the bay, Neapolitans with manners as animated as Vesuvius. Lord Mount Cashell, in velvet and embroidery, ruffles, bag, and sword, was presented to the Royal Family. Later, Lady M. and Miss Wilmot were presented to the Queen of Naples at the palace, and that evening met the Royal Family at Sir John Acton's ball. "The Queen," said Miss Wilmot, "is a sturdy looking dame by no means elegant in her deportment, and trotted about in her black and blue robes, much more as if she was crying tooky, tooky, tooky after her Poultry like a housewife, than a Queen doing the dignities of her drawing room. The King looks like an overgrown Ass, tho' in his demeanour he is exceeding civil; however his face surpasses any abridgement of imbecility I ever saw in all my life. . . ."[7]

The English in Naples never budged out of their own pale except to attend the weekly balls given by the Russian Countess Skawronsky. The Mount Cashells were the only English who moved in Neapolitan society. Lady M. was amused to hear the English passing snarling sarcasms on the manners of the Neapolitans whom they did not know, for she did know them and was enchanted by their ingenuousness, good humor, and merry manners.

Every day they sent her flowers, carnations as big as pe-
onies, invitations, embossed notes, and offers of eternal
friendship. She was a great favorite among them, especially after she gave a grand ball to return their hospitality.

They attended the Prince d'Hugris's balls, where
everybody treated them as acquaintances; Prince Ruffano's
conversazioni, where ladies and gentlemen played at faro;
the Countess Skawronsky's balls, where they met English
people: Lord Beverley, Lord Grantham, Lady Hester
Stanhope, Sir William Drummond, the English ambassador, who hated the Neapolitans and they him. The
names flow through the journal: Admiral Caracciolo, the
Portuguese Minister and Madame Sa, the Spanish Ambassador and La Marquise de Mos, Citoyen Alquier, the
French ambassador, il Principe d'Avella, il Duca di Cari-
gnano, il Principe d'Arecco, Don Antonio Correade Soto-
mayor, il Principe di Piedmonte, il Principe Caramanico,
the Duchess of Campochiara, the Princess de Hesse Phil-
ipstal, Madame Falconet, and so on, and so on, and so on.

The ladies discovered that the opera at San Carlo was
more social than musical; brocaded princes moved from
box to box, the ladies blazed with diamonds like a constellation. Cakes and ices, hams, pies, and macaroni were
served in the boxes, the fashionables paying no more attention to the music than they did to the resounding
smacks of kisses, except perhaps during a principal aria
when they would look at the stage in animated delight.
The travelers, charmed with the fashion of visiting from
box to box, would return to their own box to find an
entirely new assemblage there. It was with regret that
they left Naples early in March.

At Rome they lodged in the Hotel Pio on the Piazza
di Spagna, the English ghetto of Rome, and set about
examining everything that was to be seen above- or under-

ground: St. Peter's, the Vatican, the Scala Santa, the Baths of Diocletian, the Colosseum, the ceremonies of Holy Week, the cemetery near the pyramid of Caius Cestius where heretics were buried. They called frequently in the mornings on Angelica Kauffmann, whose mild manners and voice were as charming as the fact that she was now a delicate old lady still painting. A famous Roman sight they saw, denied to subsequent travelers, was Lord Bristol, the Bishop of Derry, with a nightcap on his head and a mistress on each arm, riding in his carriage through the streets.

They spent one delightful day at Frascati calling on Henry, Cardinal Duke of York, brother to the Pretender, to whom they were presented by Cardinal Erskine. They found his Royal Highness still handsome at seventy-eight with the freshness of youth on his countenance, though he was infirm in body. At two o'clock they sat down to dinner, Lady M. and Miss Wilmot on either side of the Cardinal, the other guests being cardinals, bishops, and one Capuchin. After dinner they were shown the Duke's Chapel and its treasures, and, while the clergymen played cards, the ladies were taken to the top of the house to enjoy the prospect. "The blithesome gaiety of this pious conclave of Holy men was very pleasant and amusing," Miss Wilmot said. "I never saw a more joyous crew. . . ."[8] Before leaving, Lady Mount Cashell was presented with a medal, one side of which was engraved with a likeness of Cardinal York and the other with the words "Henry IX."

On Good Friday at four in the afternoon the Princess Borghese presented Lady Mount Cashell and Miss Wilmot to His Holiness, Pope Pius VII. They went in their carriage to the Vatican gardens, where at the end of a long avenue they saw the Pope dressed in scarlet and gold surrounded by his court. The Princess Borghese fell on her knees and kissed the Pope's toe, but when the Irish ladies bent to do the same, His Holiness with a motion of his hand prevented them from paying the tribute they gladly would have paid. Without ceremony and with the simplest, most gentlemanly manners, he led them into a pavilion where they conversed for an hour in Italian, the Pope sincerely amused at Lady Mount Cashell's desire to visit the Convent of the Capuchins and to see their cemetery. As the Pope and the cardinals escorted the ladies through the gardens to their carriage, His Holiness plucked a hyacinth and presented it to Lady Mount Cashell, desiring one of the cardinals to do the same for Miss Wilmot. He presented the ladies with prayer beads made of agate and jasper encased in gold, but for the second time he would not permit them to kiss his toe as the Princess Borghese did upon their departure.

Permission to visit the Convent of the Capuchins was duly delivered, perhaps an unprecedented permission that allowed two ladies, and heretics at that, within the cloister. "We were last of all," Miss Wilmot wrote, "conducted into the cell of the Superior, who received us with a grace, ease, and dignity so peculiar, that we cou'd think of nothing else. I never saw so striking a Being in all my life, and as he stood in his little cell, without a second chair to offer us or one single comfort or luxury of existence, his air inspired a greater reverence and admiration than all the Thrones and Potentates in Christendom."[9]

After a seven-days' journey by way of Perugia and Arezzo the travelers arrived again in Florence, having survived a slight accident which overturned them and their carriage into a pool of water by the side of the road. From Florence they made a brief excursion to Leghorn, where they attended a service at the Jewish synagogue and visited the burying place of the English. On the way back to Florence they stopped for three or four hours in Pisa to see the sights. Lady Mount Cashell had no thought that she was to spend twenty years of her life in Pisa and was to be buried in the English cemetery in Leghorn.

A great many of their Roman and Neapolitan friends were in Florence, and they were especially happy to renew their intimacy with the Princess Montemiletto. She and Miss Wilmot exchanged English and Italian lessons, the princess becoming more and more delightful as her character unfolded. Very often the ladies and the princess drove at the fashionable hour of the evening among the trees in the Cascina.

During this stay in Florence, Lady M. became the patroness of an Italian scholar, Giovanni Fabbroni, who dedicated to her his book *Degli Antichi Abitatori D'Italia . . . Indirizzati sotto gli Auspici di Miledi Margarita Giovanna Contessa di Mont Cashell . . . Firenze*, 1803. In his dedication, Fabbroni paid tribute to Ireland, to Irish scholars, to the Irish language, and to Lady Mount Cashell, who spoke Italian to perfection.

In the spring of 1803 Richard had the measles, and subsequently Lady Mount Cashell underwent a long illness, which prevented the party from rejoining the other children in France. Then on June 1 word reached Florence that war had broken out again between England and France and that an embargo had been placed on British travelers. The Mount Cashell children had been taken to Geneva; Mr. Egan, their tutor, was imprisoned by the French. Consternation and rumors broke out among the English. What was to become of them? Some said they were to be evacuated by sea from Leghorn to perish in the Bay of Biscay—if they were not taken by pirates. "Ransoms were speculated upon; chains and dungeons glanced at; Gentlemen went off in disguise at the peril of their lives; ladies fainted; the Duchess of Cumberland flew to the Pope's dominions," etc., etc.[10]   The Mount Cashells wanted to be reunited with their children, but it was utterly impossible for gentlemen to return to England.   A Mrs. Clifford allowed Miss Wilmot to join her party which left for home by way of Germany on July 10.   "The miseries of the last few days previous to my parting with Lady Mount Cashell, I will cover with a Pall," Miss Wilmot wrote; "two years uninterrupted happiness in her society, was obliterated by the anguish of separation, and the morning of my departure, I never more earnestly wished for anything, than that, even by so long a spell of pleasure, I had not incur'd the trials to which I then became a victim."[11]

The Mount Cashells were successful in reuniting the family and taking the children to Rome.   There they put Lord Kilworth, their eldest son, into Saint Isidore's College to be educated by the Irish Franciscans.   Father James MacCormack was Guardian; the distinguished Brother Richard Hayes of Wexford became Kilworth's good friend.   When the parents discovered before it was too late that their son was becoming a Roman in his heart and would willingly suffer martyrdom in the cause of Catholicism, they removed him at once from the convent. What would it profit Lord Kilworth to become a Roman and suffer the loss of his estate?[12]

Lady Mount Cashell found the English in Rome especially dull.   Most of them never mingled with the Italians, and some never left the neighborhood of the Piazza di Spagna.   The gentlemen were better at billiards than they were at any exercise of the intellect. There was not an intellectually stimulating person among them until the arrival, early in 1804, of a young Irish gentleman, Mr. George William Tighe, a member of the Tighe family of Rosanna, County Wicklow.

MRS. MASON

CHAPTER 7.

THE DEPARTURE OF Catherine Wilmot in July of 1803 left a vacuum in Lady Mount Cashell's life. For two years she had enjoyed the intellectual and sympathetic companionship of a spirited and intelligent young woman. Deprived of that companionship, she could not turn to her husband, whose lack of intellectual interests and whose aversion to everything she thought worthwhile made him appear daily more contemptible. For over six months she endured this life diverted only by the fashionable society which she detested. Under these circumstances, a matron of thirty-one, she met George William Tighe, who was twenty-eight. From the beginning she found that he was "interesting" and "appeared to advantage."

There is every reason to believe that they had known each other, at least casually, in Dublin during the 1790's: their fathers were both members of Parliament; his mother, Anna Tighe, was the prominent founder and director of an Irish home for orphans; he and Lady Mount Cashell's brothers had been students together at Eton; he was considered to be "very handsome & a great Beau"[1] in Dublin society before the Union. One feels certain that the Tighes, the Kingstons, and the Mount Cashells were acquainted.

J. D. Herbert, Irish portrait painter and clubman, devotes two chapters of his gossipy book, *Irish Varieties*, to a discussion of Edward Tighe, the father of George William. Herbert writes, "Mr. Edward Tighe, of the county of Wicklow, a gentleman of high family, had imbibed an early taste for English reading and speaking, *free from Irish accent*; this taste he cultivated so highly as to become the best English reader of his day. . . . no party, however select, could be considered perfect without Mr. E. Tighe."[2]

At that time Edward Tighe was a barrister and first commissioner in the Office of Impressed Accounts. Herbert testifies as to the conviviality of his hospitality by describing a dinner party given at the Tighe home on Leeson Street. The guests were several gentlemen; the hostess was the housekeeper, Mrs. Jackson, "a fine comely woman, of a large model, very like the Antique of Ariadne, which she was called, as a pet name. Her little son and my young soldier sat beside each other, at a small table. . . ."[3] Mr. Tighe told his guests the story of his stage-struck life —how he had devoted his talents to the acquisition of a perfect English accent at Eton; how he had studied law to please his father, but had taken rooms near David Garrick, had attended the theater every night, and had become Garrick's close friend. (Another member of Dr. Johnson's circle with whom he was intimate was Sir Joshua Reynolds, who gave him a presentation copy of one of his books.)[4]

Sir Brooke Boothby, baronet and poet, included poems to Edward Tighe and his son in Sir Brooke's *Sorrows: Sacred to the Memory of Penelope*, 1796. The poem dedicated to George reads, in much-abridged form:

Dear George, my long-loved Edward's gracious son;

Whether we climb old Dubris awful steep, . . .
Or further go, where lucid Leman shines . . .
Still to sweet Ashbourne turns my weary mind . . .
There shalt thou strew with sweets my lifeless clay;
And there thy tears bedew my recent urn.

George was born in Dublin in 1776 and at the age of
nine was sent off to Eton, where he remained until he was
eighteen, distinguishing himself particularly in the study
of Latin and Greek. After leaving Eton in 1794 he joined
the militia, choosing a less tranquil life than that of a
scholar. We hear of him fighting in the rebel English
colonies in America, and we hear of him as a captain in
the Seventh Dragoon Guards after he had returned to
Ireland. The life of the militia lost its appeal, and we
find him in London registered as a law student at Lincoln's
Inn in 1800.[5] His father, too, had gone to England after
the Union, in infirm health as he approached sixty.
In 1802 he died, leaving George his estate without any
limitations.[6] His Italian descendants have documents,
sometimes only scraps of paper, which give part of his
story: receipts, account books, a passport, a few letters, a
journal (much of which he seems to have destroyed),
some moral essays which he wrote for the instruction of his
children, one or two papers marked in pencil "burn" and
others marked "may be saved for the children."

The estate he inherited consisted of 458 acres in the
County Athlone rented to middlemen named Thomas and
William Timms, who paid him £482 a year. They in
turn rented to occupiers with names like Gallagher and
FitzGerald, or Michael Cormack who had twenty-nine
acres, James Laughlin who had thirty-eight, and Pat
Martin who had seventeen. But George also inherited
his father's debts. These included an annuity of £100 to

Mr. Jackson, 25 Rue de Cléry, Paris, and items such as
£100 owed to a tailor named Crayton near Abbey Street
in Dublin.[7]

After his father's death, George, still the handsome
beau, went to Italy. A few sentences on an unburned page
supply a clue. "About the Age of six & twenty," he
wrote, "soon after my coming into Italy, my thoughts took
a new turn, my pursuits became gradually better, & I have
ended by making Health, Study, & Oeconomy my principal
objects in life. One of the first things I learnt upon my
arrival in Italy was a contempt of what is called Fashion.
The wretched dress, Equipage & Furniture of the Italians
evidently excites as much Emulation in some, & affords as
much self-complacency to others, as the same objects
carried to perfection could possibly do. The *dull comedy*
of the Italian world appeared to me odious, because the
Actors. . . ." This marks the end of a page; the next
does not exist.[8]

When he arrived in Rome early in 1804 he still
mingled with the fashionables, even though Italian society
was to him odious. On April 30 of that year he was elected
to the *Arcadi Pastori*, an Italian literary society founded
in 1690 of which Goethe was another foreign member.
On August 27, Lady Mount Cashell gave birth to her
third daughter, Elizabeth Anne. Before the year was out
she discovered that she was in love with the man who
from the first appeared to her as "interesting," and she
discovered also that neither of them "had sufficient resolution to withstand a strong passion. . . ."

Yet she continued to live with Lord M. and had
enough resolution to start with him and the children, the
servants and tutors, on the homeward journey to Ireland
by way of Germany. Before her lay a lifetime with a
man she detested in a country where she had witnessed the

trial and death of her father and the collapse of her every republican hope. Behind her lay Italy and the man whom she loved. The struggle that she made to return to Ireland and to do what she thought right was a sincere struggle, but her will was weaker than her love. In 1805 Lord Mount Cashell continued on his return trip to Ireland with the children, leaving her alone in Germany to face years of anxieties, difficulties, and misfortune. She never saw him again. Mary Smith, her maid, remained with her.

She could no longer be known as Lady Mount Cashell, although this deprivation caused her no regret, nor could she be known as Mrs. Tighe. The little girl, her counterpart, in Mary Wollstonecraft's *Original Stories* had said, "I wish to be a woman and to be like Mrs. Mason." Now that she was a woman free of the title she never loved, she could take the name of Mason and, in that middle class for which she had always sighed, dedicate herself to a life that would have had the approval of her former governess, with a man who was both her lover and her companion. Her intellectual energies she would devote to completing projects which Mary Wollstonecraft had planned but had not lived to realize: a series of books for children and a book for mothers on the physical education of children.

Lord M. proceeded on his way to Ireland and, according to one report, was taken prisoner by Napoleon.[9] When he did reach Ireland, he gave up his Dublin home, Mount Cashell House on St. Stephen's Green, which was subsequently occupied by J. P. Curran. Memoirs of the period contain occasional references to his presence in Dublin and London.

Mrs. Mason then became, in her own words, "a vagabond on the face of the earth,"[10] precisely where we do not know, although she was back in London by 1807. There were a great many doors in London that were closed to her, nor would she want to open them. One open door belonged to William Godwin. His household consisted of himself, Mary Wollstonecraft's daughter Fanny Imlay, his own daughter Mary Godwin, his wife's son Charles Clairmont, and her daughter Jane, whom we may call (as she later called herself) Claire Clairmont. In addition the Godwins had a boy of their own, William. Supporting himself, his wife, and five children was perhaps Godwin's major problem, especially after his wife had talked him into opening a publishing house and bookshop for young children.

This house published The Juvenile Library, to which we owe the Lambs' *Tales from Shakespeare*, Lamb's *Voyages of Ulysses*, Hazlitt's *English Grammar*, and the English edition of *Swiss Family Robinson*. At first the business was run under the name of Baldwin (for who would allow children to handle books stamped with the name of William Godwin?), but in 1807 the business and the ménage were moved to Skinner Street, Holborn, and began operating there under the name of M. J. Godwin. It was fitting that Mrs. Godwin's initials should be used, for, after all, she did most of the work.

Mrs. Godwin was a managing woman, glib and fussy, who alienated many of the philosopher's old friends. "Pitifully artificial," "deceitful," "damned disagreeable," "infernal devil," "pustule of vanity," "that bitch" are only a few of the words that Godwin's literary friends applied to her. Yet she must have had some virtues: Godwin loved her, and Mrs. Mason seems to have been fond of her and the children.

Here are some of the relevant, cryptic entries which Godwin made in his journal for the year 1807:

July 9   Call on Taylor & Johnson & C Mountcashel
July 21   C Mountcashel at tea: & tks sup: Hazlitt calls
July 26   Aprés diner, C Mountcashel, £200
July 27   C Mountcashell at tea
Sep 25   Call on C Mountcashel
Sept 28   Curran breakfasts: call w. him on North,
          O'Brien, & Mountcashel
Oct   1   C. Mountcashell calls
Oct   2   C Mountcashell M Lamb & TT call
Oct   6   Mrs. Taylor & C Mountcashel call
Oct 15   C Mountcashel dines
Oct 18   Call on Mountcashell (w. Curran)
Oct 19   C Mountcashel dines
Oct 21   C Mountcashel dines
Oct 22   C Mountcashell dines
Oct 25   Curran calls, talk of CM
Dec 30   Old Daniel published[11]

Interpreting these entries includes some guesswork.
The facts are that Mrs. Mason was in London during
July, September, and October; that she saw much of Godwin, who still referred to her as the Countess of Mount
Cashell; that she met J. P. Curran. (When she was not
in London she lived, at least part of the time, at Marlow,
the little village up the Thames where Shelley was to reside a decade later.) Does the entry of July 26 mean
that two hundred pounds changed hands? Godwin
scholars feel that in any such exchange Godwin would be
the recipient. Do the entries of September 28 and October 18 mean that Godwin was in touch with Lord Mount
Cashell, and does the presence of lawyer Curran signify
that the gentlemen were arranging some financial settlement for Mrs. Mason? The year ends with a fact that
needs no conjecture, the publication of Mrs. Mason's

*Stories of Old Daniel: or Tales of Wonder and Delight
Containing Narratives of Foreign Countries and Manners,
and Designed As an Introduction to the Study of Voyages,
Travels, and History in General,* the second volume in
Godwin's Juvenile Library, priced at three shillings and
sixpence.

Old Daniel was a real man, between ninety and a
hundred, who lived in a little village in Ireland with his
daughter Susan, a dog, a cat, and a starling. The description of his house and garden facing the village green
makes him sound very much like a resident of Kingston
College. Every Sunday the boys of the village, aged nine
to thirteen, would gather outside Old Daniel's door and
listen to his stories; and they were wonderful stories, for
Old Daniel had been a soldier who had had wonderful ex-
periences. The tales have about them a period flavor of
didacticism, and any little boy who listened to them was
bound to be improved. The author, Mrs. Mason, found
it expedient to alter some of Daniel's stories and to add
others, recognizable as having been derived from her own
experience: "The Robber's Cave" owes something to the
caves at Mitchelstown; "The Man-Hater" is much like
the story that little Sophé told at Fontainebleau; and
"Father Giacomo" is a development of the experience
the Irish travelers had with the banditti at the sinister
inn outside Pavia. The author's purpose was "to encourage a love of reading—the most independent of all
employments and the most durable of all pleasures."
New stories were added as subsequent editions appeared:
a second in 1810, a third in 1813, a seventh in 1820, a
twelfth in 1843, a thirteenth in 1850, and a fourteenth in
1868.

In 1809, Mrs. Mason gave birth to a child (fittingly,
for the original Mrs. Mason, a daughter) whom she

named Anna Laura Georgina Tighe and whom she called
Laurette. During 1810 and 1811 she was corresponding
with Godwin, and during October, November, and December of 1812 a "C M" paid many calls on the Godwins. If
these letters mean the "Countess of Mount Cashell,"
Mrs. Mason met Percy Shelley as early as 1812, for,
while C M was calling on October 7, Shelley came to pay
a visit.

During the first seven years of their life together,
Mrs. Mason and Mr. Tighe had financial difficulties, as
indicated by their accounts and receipts. Mary Smith went
unpaid until the sum due her amounted to £400. They
owed Lady de Clifford £900 with interest, the whole to
be paid by December, 1814. But in 1812 bills were
being paid, and it seems likely that Mrs. Mason began
then to receive her annuity, which amounted to roughly
a thousand pounds, certainly through Lord Mount Cashell, for the annuity ceased at his death and was renewed
through the agency of his son, the third earl.[12]

George Tighe proceeded honorably and efficiently to
pay off his debts and the debts of his father. The Reverend James W. Sterling, Rector of Athlone, was instructed "to pay unto Robert Hughes of Cheltenham in
the County of Gloucester Gentleman" all the sums due
to the creditors. He himself was in Dublin in January
of 1813 looking for the tailor to whom his father owed
£100. "I certainly shall not go out of the country," he
wrote to his agent in 1814, "without having assigned a
satisfactory provision for the payment of the bond due in
December."[13] Finally, the couple were free of their debts
and received from their agents the long-awaited note,
"Permit us to return you our thanks for the confidence
placed in us as well as for the very handsome & honorable

manner in which you have been pleased to liquidate the Debts of your late Father."[14]

Mrs. Mason had long wanted to leave England for some quiet place in Italy both because of her desire for seclusion and her need for a warmer climate. The threat of consumption, which Mary Wollstonecraft had feared when Mrs. Mason was fifteen and which was to harass her later years, was already giving her trouble; in England she had to spend four months of the year with windows shut, fighting the cold and damp. By the summer of 1814, the couple and their five-year-old daughter, Laurette, were ready to leave for Italy. Mrs. Mason's income was assured; Mr. Tighe's rents in Ireland were to be collected by their friend Charles Hamilton and turned over to Coutts and Company for transmission.

The city of Pisa seemed exactly what they wanted for their permanent residence. It was a tranquil, sleepy city, depopulated from its one hundred and twenty thousand citizens in the days of the Republic to eighteen thousand in 1814. Shelley thought that nothing could surpass a sunset at Pisa, and Leopardi found the Lung'Arno more beautiful than anything he had seen in Florence, Milan, or Rome. More telling than the city's tranquil beauty was its reputation as a health resort, particularly for consumptives. The head of the faculty of surgery at the University of Pisa was Andrea Vaccà Berlinghieri, "one of the great names in Italy," the *Dio della Medicina*," whose presence in Pisa brought many patients there.

The Masons spent some time in London taking care of details. Mr. Tighe had to get a passport and Mrs. Mason had to find a maid, for Mary Smith, who had been faithful for so many years, could not bring herself to go abroad again. At her London hotel, Mrs. Mason found an honest and affectionate English girl, Betsy Parker, who thought that she would like to go.[15]

On July 28, Robert Stewart, *Vicomte* Castlereagh, issued a passport to *Monsieur* George William Tighe, *Gentilhomme Anglais*, asking foreign states to allow him, his wards, and baggage safe passage as he traveled on the Continent.[16] On August 7 Mrs. Mason paid her last call on the Godwins.[17] Then the passport guides us on their journey. On August 19 they were at Calais; on September 1 in Paris. Thence they went to Chambéry, Turin, Bologna, Florence, and finally Pisa, where they arrived on October 18 and where they were to spend the remainder of their lives. Soon they were established in the Casa Silva, a comfortable house on the south side of the Arno with a small garden shaded by walnut trees.

In this house the couple lived a tranquil life, Mrs. Mason caring for their daughter and continuing her writing, Mr. Tighe dividing his time between his library and his garden. He concentrated his agricultural studies principally on the potato, which he grew both in the ground and in pots. Before his time, the Tuscan potato had been a neglected and ignoble vegetable without a hint of the place it was subsequently to occupy in the Italian diet. At first he imported varieties of the potato from many countries and experimented scrupulously with their cultivation; he then published his results, providing Italian posterity with lasting benefits.[18] At the time, his Italian neighbors thought him an eccentric, growing potatoes in pots.[19]

The Masons were very poor after paying their debts and taking the long journey to Pisa, and they could afford only an inexpensive woman to assist Betsy with the cooking. After suffering from a series of trollops, Mrs. Mason tried the Foundling Hospital, which provided her with a girl who looked like the offspring of a German soldier and a street walker. This girl was not satisfactory either, and Betsy went to the hospital to pick a colleague herself. Mrs. Mason was in too delicate health to go, being pregnant and threatened with a miscarriage. When Mrs. Mason later noticed that Betsy was scratching inordinately, examination showed that she had acquired the itch from the German servant and only hospitalization could cure it. A kind old nun in the hospital took a great interest in the sick Betsy, and the cured Betsy became not only a Catholic but a nun as well, Suora Ancilla of the order of St. Clare. She was assigned work in the hospital, where she was highly respected, where she prayed for the conversion of Mrs. Mason, and whence she was sometimes granted permission to visit Casa Silva.[20]

Back in Ireland, Charles Hamilton was working in the Tighe interests, not confining his efforts to the collection of rents. In August of 1815 he was successful in securing a pension on the Civil Lists by which George Tighe would receive four hundred pounds a year for life and in return would supply the treasury with a sample of his signature four times a year. His annual income, after paying the annuity to Mr. Jackson and the interest on some small debts, amounted to six hundred pounds.[21]

The year 1815 brought joy and sorrow. The Honorable Robert Moore, his mother's favorite, was seriously wounded at Waterloo on July 18. On June 20 at ten in the morning, a second daughter, Catherine Elizabeth Tighe, was born,[22] and now Mrs. Mason, just like the Mrs. Mason of Mary Wollstonecraft's *Original Stories*, had two little girls to care for and educate. This second daughter they called Nerina.

The family associated with Italians rather than with English. Dr. Vaccà was their friend and physician; Professor and Mrs. Francesco Tantini called and were called upon. The girls had tutors to teach them music and French and Italian. From the first it was apparent that Laurette was to be beautiful and robust, Nerina delicate and serious. One cannot but envy the serene existence that the family finally achieved after years of political and social unhappiness.

George Tighe's little moral essays show that he agreed with Mrs. Mason on most subjects such as society, religion, and dress. One essay describing the life he would like to have led reads very much like the life he did lead. He was able to conclude a brief autobiography with the words, "Certain it is that after many storms we now enjoy as much happiness as falls to the lot of most people. But let it be remembered that this has been gained after many years of doubt and anxiety & that generally speaking an illegitimate connection is as miserable as it is criminal."[23]

CHAPTER 8.

ON THE DAY THAT Viscount Castlereagh issued a passport to George William Tighe, Gentleman—that is, on July 28, 1814—another, more momentous event took place: Percy Shelley, the poet, eloped with Mary Godwin. A curious circumstance was that he took along his wife's step-sister, Claire Clairmont, but did not take along his wife, Harriet Westbrook Shelley—though it needs to be said that he later invited Harriet to join them. Mary was not quite seventeen, Claire eight months younger, and Shelley twenty-two.

At four in the morning Mary and Claire slipped out of their father's house on Skinner Street to join Shelley, who was waiting with a post chaise at the corner of Hatton Garden, and the three galloped off to Dover, the sea, and freedom. An hour later Godwin found the note his daughter had left for him; Mrs. Godwin took the next mail coach post-post-haste to Dover, pursuing not Mary Godwin but her own daughter Claire. Godwin wrote in his journal "*Five in the Morning*" and underscored the words.[1] The absconders reached Dover at four in the afternoon and wisely engaged a small boat manned by two fishermen to take them across the Channel. Otherwise they would have had to wait until the next day for the packet. Instead of the two-hour trip they were promised, they had a dreadful, seasick crossing which lasted through the night. The next morning they were in Calais resting at Dessein's Hotel.

In the evening word was brought to Shelley that a fat lady had arrived charging that Shelley had run off with her daughter. Claire spent the night with her mother. The next day she announced her decision to remain with the lovers, and Mrs. Godwin departed without a word. Shelley and the girls left the same evening for Boulogne and Paris.

Back in England, Mrs. Godwin began writing letters imploring Mrs. Mason to look after Claire, should the trio go to Pisa, and to persuade her to leave Shelley. Mrs. Godwin wrote* that at Calais Shelley was asked whether he was in love with Claire. "No," he replied, "I am not in the least in love with her; but she is a nice little girl, and her mother is such a vulgar, commonplace woman, without an idea of philosophy, I do not think she is a proper person to form the mind of a young girl."[2] London gossips were saying that Godwin had sold the two girls to Shelley: Mary for eight hundred pounds and Claire for seven hundred. Mrs. Mason replied, "The impression you gave me of Mary makes me think her conduct perfectly natural—she only acted like a person who cares for nothing but herself; but I am surprised at [Claire] from whom you had taught me to expect something better."[3]

But the trio did not go to Pisa. Instead they toured France, Switzerland, Germany, and Holland, returning to London after six weeks. The Godwins would have nothing on earth to do with Shelley, except that Godwin would take money from him, and Mrs. Godwin would

* Mrs. Godwin's letters exist only in treacherous copies made by Claire.

parade in front of Shelley's house on Margaret Street, trying to peer in the window.

Shelley was not unused to tribulations: at Eton he was rebellious and miserable and called "mad Shelley"; at Oxford he published a pamphlet called *The Necessity of Atheism* and was expelled; at home his father, Sir Timothy Shelley, raged at the monstrous behavior of his genius son. But Shelley's remaining, eventful years brought greater woe. In November, 1814, Harriet, the wife from whom he had separated, gave birth to a son. In February Mary Godwin gave birth to a seven months' child; two weeks later she found the child dead in the bed beside her. Then, unknown to Shelley, his beloved Mary had an affair with his friend Thomas Jefferson Hogg, while Shelley was being pursued by creditors. In January of the next year (1816), a son, William, was born to Shelley and Mary. In October Fanny Imlay, Mary's half-sister, committed suicide. In November Harriet Shelley committed suicide. The next month Shelley married Mary, and in September of the next year (1817) Mary gave birth to a daughter, Clara. In March, Lord Chancellor Eldon had given judgment against Shelley in his suit to obtain possession of Harriet's children.

During these years, Claire Clairmont was not idle. Like Mary, Claire had fallen in love with a poet, the notorious and wicked Lord Byron. She wrote to him, signing her letter E. Trefusis, declaring her love and offering him her unstained reputation and infinite capacity for affection. Byron was not impressed. She wrote again "on business of peculiar importance." Byron was bored. But the eighteen-year-old Claire was so persistent that when Byron left England in April, 1816, she was pregnant with his daughter Allegra. She persuaded Shelley and Mary to spend the summer in Switzerland with Byron,

Lady Mount Cashell
*From a physionotrace engraving made in Paris
by Edme Quenedey*

Lady Mount Cashell

From a drawing by an unknown artist

she going along, of course. The next January, back in
England, Claire gave birth to Byron's daughter.

This is briefly the background of the Shelley ménage
that set out for Italy in March of 1818, the month that
Mary published her novel *Frankenstein*. The party included Shelley and Mary with their children William and
Clara, Claire Clairmont with her daughter Allegra, and
two nurses: the Swiss Élise and the English Milly.
Claire's plan was to turn Allegra over to Lord Byron for
the obvious advantages of rank and wealth with which he
could provide the child. Byron's terms were so harsh—
Claire was to give up all claim to Allegra and never try
to see her again—that Shelley attempted to dissuade her
from parting with her daughter. But Claire was un-
selfishly stubborn, and the little girl was sent to her self-
indulgent father in Venice on the day after her mother's
twentieth birthday.

Shelley's party moved about Italy: Parma, Modena,
Bologna, Florence, Rome, Naples. At Rome Shelley
thought the English burying-place the most solemn and
beautiful cemetery he had ever beheld. Tragedy still
pursued him. In September their daughter Clara died
in Venice. The next June their son William died in
Rome. The autumn of 1819 found them, childless, in
Leghorn. Mary was pregnant, and Shelley wanted to
take her to Florence where she could be under the care
of Mr. John Bell, a famous Scottish surgeon whom the
Shelleys had known in Rome. On September 30, Shelley,
Mary, and Claire left Leghorn for Florence. On the way,
they stopped for a day in Pisa.

Mrs. Mason was at home when the party arrived. Her
quiet life was devoted to the care of her two daughters,
research on a medical book she was writing, and the run-
ning of what might be called a dispensary for poor sick

Pisans who sought her help and advice. The Shelley who came to the door of Casa Silva was a slender, slightly stooped gentleman, with dark, unkempt hair, expressive eyes, fair complexion, and fine features, with a simple, earnest way of talking and a natural good breeding. The warm welcome Mrs. Mason extended to him may be attributed not only to the admiration she had for his poetry but also to the love she felt for the husband of Mary Wollstonecraft's daughter. It was refreshing for him to find a rooted friend of sound common sense after years of vagabondage, tragedy, and uncertainty. Unfortunately Mrs. Mason could not give the Shelleys letters to any friends in Florence, for the Florentines she had known as Lady Mount Cashell would not be likely to welcome friends of Mrs. Mason.

But she could help them find a servant, Carolina, eighteen years old, a friend of Betsy Parker's, chaste and honest—a chaste maid being rarer than an honest one. Mrs. Mason instructed them how to manage an Italian servant: Carolina was to receive wages of three *francesconi* a month out of which she was to buy bread and wine, she should be allowed time to attend mass, and fasting food should be provided on fast days. Once when Mary complimented Mrs. Mason on her common sense she replied, "I cannot boast of any of that cool good sense which is bestowed on some people at their birth—hard experience has beat into me the little I possess."[4]

On November 12, Mary gave birth to a son, whom she called Percy Florence. Immediately Shelley notified Mrs. Mason, sending along also a bit of bad news from London. Godwin was again in serious financial difficulties and expected, as usual, to be rescued by Shelley. For the remainder of his life, every joy Shelley experienced was to be tainted by whines from Godwin; and poor, easily depressed Mary was to be made ill by the self-pitying appeals of her father. Mrs. Mason replied to Shelley on November 14.

"I wish you both joy most sincerely of this happy event," she wrote, "and hope my dear Mary and her little boy will be soon strong enough to move to Pisa, the climate of which I have no doubt will be more favourable to all of you than that of Florence. A thousand thanks for your kind inquiries about my poor invalid [Mr. Tighe's rheumatism was troubling him], who is so well recovered as to have been once out in a carriage, and is now only confined to the house by the weather, which is very justly called 'scellerato'; but, by what I know of Florence, I am sure it is still worse there. I am very sorry for the bad news you have received, I had a letter from Mrs. Godwin a few days since, in which she hints mysteriously at something disagreeable that she has to tell me, which I suppose to be this circumstance. I believe you are right in not letting her know of everything that happens. She thinks Charles [Clairmont, Claire's brother who had joined the Shelleys] has not met you. She says she 'is glad that Mary is near such a kind matronly friend as Mrs. Gisborne' in her present situation. This I think is said with a design of knowing whether I have seen you; but you may be sure I shall say nothing on the subject. She writes in low spirits, and gives a very bad account of her health. What is Charles going to do at Vienna? I do not exactly understand from his Mother's letter, but have written to a friend of mine [Catherine Wilmot], whose sister is there, to desire her to do everything in her power to serve any person of that name who may appear there as a teacher of the English and other languages. As she is the wife of a person attached to the British Embassy, she will probably hear of him, and have means of being useful to him. I should be glad to know more about his plans, that I may write less in the dark next time. Your kind remembrance of Laurette flatters her parents extremely. She is rejoiced to hear of the birth of the little child, which she longs to see, and desires me to tell you to come here soon. Your plans, I should suppose, would require much reflection, for health is not to be sacrificed lightly; but there are many months till spring; and I only hope Mr. Godwin's affairs may get better before that time. I flatter myself that, after this uncommonly bad weather, we shall have a fine winter. I continue (for me) remarkably well; but my health is always capricious. I hope to hear from one or other of my correspondents soon again, and am very much obliged for the friendly attention of both to theirs, / Very faithfully, / Margaretta.

"P.S.—Pray remember me to your companion [Claire], and tell her Laurette practises the pianoforte with more than usual attention, in hopes of amusing her when she comes here. I should not forget to say that my little Nerina often asks, 'Dove sono gli Signori Inglesi?' "

In a second postscript, Mrs. Mason asked Shelley's help in forwarding to her a parcel from Rome. "I will not make apologies," she concluded, "for they do not seem to me to accord with the frankness of your or my character."[5] The straightforward letters which Mrs. Mason wrote to Shelley and Mary during the next few weeks indicate the interests and the doings of the correspondents. The following letter, undated, was probably written within a week or two of the first. Mary, encouraged by the success of *Frankenstein,* was gathering material on Castruccio, Prince of Lucca, for her second novel, *Valperga.* "My dear Sir," Mrs. Mason wrote to Shelley:

"I deferred answering your letter till this post in

hopes of being able to send some recommendations for your friend [Charles] at Vienna, in which I have been disappointed; and I have now also a letter from my dear Mary; so I will answer both together. It gives me great pleasure to hear such a good account of the little boy and his mother. If you are friends to the vaccine, and can have it where you are, I advise you not to delay, as it is sometimes difficult to be obtained in this country. I am sorry to perceive that your visit to Pisa will be so much retarded; but I admire Mary's courage and industry. I sincerely regret that it is not in my power to be of service to her in this undertaking. I have not been in Florence, except once, *en passant,* these fifteen years [that is, on her way from London to Pisa in 1814], and the few people I knew there [in 1803] have probably no recollection of me, nor if they had would it (for many and weighty reasons) be prudent to recall my name to their remembrance. All I can say is, that when you have got all you can there (where I suppose the manuscript documents are chiefly to be found), and that you come to this place, I have scarcely any doubt of being able to obtain for you many books on the subject which interests you. Probably everything in print which relates to it is as easy to be had here as at Florence. In regard to Charles, I can only advise him to call on Mrs. Bradford, wife of the Ambassador's Chaplain at Vienna, and if she has not heard anything of him, let him say that he had been given to understand that her sister, Miss Wilmot, had written to recommend him to her protection as a teacher of English, &c, &c. I have never seen Mrs. Bradford; but there was a time I would have given him a letter to her. At present, I can only make it a point with her sister, one of my oldest and most constant friends, to desire she will serve him, and this I have already done. I have had no answer to my letter, therefore cannot say that she has written to Mrs. Bradford, though I feel little doubt of her having done so. Charles must not mention me.

"I am very sorry indeed to think that Mr. Godwin's affairs are in such a bad way, and think he would be much happier if he had nothing to do with trade; but I am afraid he would not be comfortable out of England. You who are young do not mind the thousand little wants that men of his age are not habituated to; and I, who have been so many years a vagabond on the face of the earth, have long since forgotten them; but I have seen people of my age much discomposed at the absence of long-accustomed trifles; and though philosophy supports in great matters, it seldom vanquishes the small every-dayisms of life. I say this that Mary may not urge her Father too much to leave England. It may sound odd, but I can't help thinking that Mrs. Godwin would enjoy a tour in foreign countries more than he would. The physical inferiority of women sometimes teaches them to support or overlook little inconveniences better than men.

"In spite of this 'stravagantissimo' weather, Mr. T[ighe] continues to gather strength, and goes out in a carriage in cold days without injury. Such a season as this I have never seen, though I have passed eight years of my life in Italy, and five of them at Pisa. I do not now venture to say whether Mr. Shelley would find the climate of Pisa better than that of Florence; it used to be much better; but this is very properly called a *stagione mala*, and therefore perhaps you have better weather than we have. We are all much flattered by your kind remembrance of Laurette and Nerina, who are both very impatient to see the little new child. A thousand thanks for your kind promises of books. When you have done with them, let me know, and I will make [the] Procaccino [messenger] (who went to you with those I sent) call for them. Newspapers from England will soon be very interesting, but merely as an account of a new puppet-show. I expect no good. Are there many English in Florence? Here there are very few as yet, and I do not hear of any that are expected. Do not, however, fail to let me know some time before you come, and tell me what sort of a lodging you wish for, that I may find out all that are to be had. I begin to fear you will not come this winter. Kindest wishes to you all, from yours very faithfully and sincerely, / M. Mason."[6]

Other letters are concerned with Shelley's health and provide the benefit of Mrs. Mason's experience. "I have tried many climates for my health & have found this the best & Rome the next," she wrote. "Naples I found abominable & I never suffered so much from the cold as at Naples."[7] The climate at Marlow she had found extremely unwholesome; yet it had agreed with Mr. Tighe. She couldn't recommend Vaccà too highly. Other letters show concern for the fate of a manuscript she had sent to Mrs. Godwin for a new volume, *Continuation of the Stories of Old Daniel*. In another letter she asks Mary to inquire of Mrs. Gisborne in Leghorn whether there would be any children sent from Leghorn to an English boarding school in Pisa. She hoped that two respectable young women she knew in England would establish a school in Pisa.[8] One of them was Miss Mathilda Field.

On Tuesday, January 11, Mary wrote inviting Laurette to pay a visit to Florence.[9] The Shelleys would go to Pisa themselves at the end of the month, and Laurette could return with them. Shelley was not well. Reviewers of his poetry had been venomous; English politics in the last year of George III, the "old, mad, blind, despised, and dying king," seemed especially hateful to

Shelley's extreme liberalism. Viscount Castlereagh, who had (in Mrs. Mason's view) cut the throat of his native Ireland by engineering the Union, was now (in Shelley's view) cutting the throats of the English. Mrs. Mason replied immediately to Mary's letter.

      "Pisa, Friday, [January] 14, 1819 [for 1820].

    "Many thanks, my dear Mary, for all your kind attentions, and particularly your invitation to Laurette, by which honour she cannot profit. You will perhaps think me very weak when I confess to you that, accustomed as I am to have her always sleeping in my room, or the next to it, I fear when on wakening in the night I should recollect that she was far from me, it would at this moment have too strong an effect on my shattered nerves. Be assured, however, that I am thoroughly sensible of your friendly offer, and if she was a little older, and I a little stronger, I should probably be very glad to accept it. She has at present a slight cold, which affects her eyes, so that the order of the day is idleness. My poor invalid [Mr. Tighe] is better than when I wrote last, and even a slight improvement in such weather as this is very encouraging. The ground is covered with snow, and to-day the sun has had no power whatever. I am tolerably well, though the cold has given me a nervous headache, for a few hours, two or three times lately. I am very sorry to hear such a bad account of Mr. Shelley, and fear that the interest he takes in the political state of England is very injurious to his health. I speak feelingly on this subject, as my nerves have never recovered the shake they got about twenty years ago on a similar occasion. Late events have not surprised me, as I have long been convinced that if Ministers proposed to pass a Bill to prohibit men from walking on two legs, the great majority of the Parliament would instantly pop down on their hands and feet. And this is but a beginning. So that Mr. Shelley ought to endeavour to turn his thoughts from what he cannot mend, and what is only likely to produce new subjects of vexation. Since my country sank never to rise again, I have been a cool politician; but I cannot forget how I once felt, and can still sympathize with those capable of similar feelings. By the by, it may perhaps cause you to see what struck me as a *prophecy*, in looking over an old Anti-Union pamphlet which I found amongst a parcel of rubbish last summer. In reply to some honours and advantages pointed out by the writer it wishes to confute, the author says: 'I cannot perceive what advantage it could be to Ireland to have *a servile, artful, and ambitious native of that country pursuing his own interest* in the *British Cabinet,* nor how it would benefit our island to have him reproached with being an Irishman. Would this produce any commercial advantages to our cities? Would this occasion any civilization in our provinces? Would the *prostituted talents of a selfish and crafty schemer* redound to our honour, or add to our prosperity?' The date of this pamphlet is June 1799, a time at which no one guessed what Lord C[astlereagh] would arrive at. Many thanks for 'Galignani' [the English language newspaper published in Paris], but don't send it by the post any more; I will send the Procaccino. I have no Bible with the Apocrypha, but I have the Apocrypha by itself, which I will send if possible to-morrow, and Laurette will also send you some of her books. The 'Debates' are in one point of view rather droll; but the French Deputy, who 'complained of an excess of religion, which disturbed the peace of the country,' seems to me a better sort of person than any of the English speakers. I don't think one of the Opposition would have had courage to say that in Parliament. Travelling now is out of the question; but perhaps Mr. Shelley would suffer less here than at Florence. I am glad to perceive he thinks of consulting Vaccà; at all events it can do no harm to hear what he has to say on the subject. From May till September is the season for the Baths of Pisa; and as half the bathers go from hence every morning, there is no necessity whatever for living at the Bagni; they are half-way between Pisa and the country-house we had, from whence I went the three summers I was there; and if we have occasion for them this summer, we shall go from hence every day; but I believe Mr. T[ighe] will be obliged to go to Casciano for a month, and that he will go without me and the children. I am very sorry to find you still suffer from low spirits. I was in hopes the little boy would have been the best remedy for that. Words of consolation are but empty sounds, for to time alone it belongs to wear out the tears of affliction. However, a woman who gives milk should make every exertion to be cheerful, on account of the child she nourishes. What have you done with Carolina? Her friends, the Nuns of Santa Chiara, are uneasy to know what is become of her, as they heard she was to come back. Is there any chance of finding me a service for the girl I mentioned to you? With a good severe mistress, I have no doubt she would become an excellent servant; but I have no talents of that sort. If nothing is to be had at Florence, I shall send her to Livorno at the end of this month. When you once determine to come here, tell me just the sort of lodgings you wish for, and I will engage to know every one of that sort for you to choose out of as soon as you arrive. The prices, I fancy, are not so high by any means as they were. I hear there are now but *five* English families, instead of *thirty-five* which I heard of last year.

"I write in haste, and have only time to send kind

remembrances to your companions, and assure you that I am yours very sincerely, / Margaretta."[10]

The next letter, written a week later on January 21, 1820, is addressed to Shelley. "My dear Sir," it begins:

"On Tuesday evening I received your letter by Carolina, and this day's post brought me Mary's of yesterday. I am very sorry to have such bad accounts of your health in both, and think you are quite right in determining to come here and consult Vaccà. I never heard one so willing to reason with a patient, or so little inclined to giving drugs. From what you say of your complaint, I think I can guess pretty nearly how he will treat you, and I am much mistaken if he orders either of the medicines you have mentioned. If I see you before he does, I will tell you *what* I guess on the subject. Mary tells me you intend to be here the latter end of this month, and I advise you not to delay, if the weather is tolerable, as I have little doubt that both the air and water of Pisa will agree with you better than those of Florence. I have already heard of two lodgings, and shall not fail to inquire about others, so that I hope you may find something suitable for about 8 or 10 zecchini per month; but I shall write to Mary on this subject in two or three days. I expected you to be amused by the *Irish prophecy*. I am sure we are *commanded* to believe many that are not half so explicit. You cannot abhor *cant* more than I do, and there is nothing that makes one so indignant as to hear it uttered by those who ought to be above it; but everybody has some relationship or connection with the shrine-makers, and therefore few are men who are not ready to cry aloud, 'Great is Diana of the Ephesians!' I have a sad opinion of the British Parliament, and really the Ministerial part appears to me the least bad; there is not so much hypocrisy on that side. I wonder whether private letters will be liable to prosecutions for libels one of these days. I should not be surprised if they were. The Box of Pandora is opening a little more and a little more every day, and God knows what will fly out of it at last. I always foresaw that the Union with Ireland would be fatal to the British Constitution. It was then that the system of corruption was first tried, and unfortunately the success then experienced has established the practice. If I was not in a hurry to return to my poor invalid (who, by the by, continues much better), I could write much on these subjects to one who can understand me; but I flatter myself we shall have time to converse one of these days, and therefore I shall only say now that I think we are very fortunate to be at this moment in this mild Tuscany, where habitual gentleness blunts all the edges of despotic power, and where so little of the miseries and oppressions of mankind are obtruded on one's notice. Thanks to you for being troubled with my goods and chattels so long. I will try to rid you of this next week, by sending one of you with the Procaccino; he has been often to call, and says he did, but I doubt it. I am very glad to hear that your little boy prospers. With every kind wish, I remain, my dear Sir, always / Yours very truly, / M."[11]

On Sunday, January 16, the severe frost was broken by a sudden thaw, and the Shelleys decided to depart as soon as possible for Pisa. At eight in the morning of January 26, the party set out by boat on the Arno. Thirty miles and five hours later they were at Empoli, whence a four-hour carriage ride brought them to Pisa at six in the evening. They lodged at the Tre Donzelle.

CHAPTER **9.**

THE NEXT DAY, Shelley and the two girls paid their respects to Mrs. Mason. She had been lining up available lodgings for them, so that two days later, after examining the available apartments, they were able to move into Casa Frasi on the Lung'Arno. Both Mary and Claire kept journals; the following pertinent extracts from Claire's show the frequency of the visits and the intimacy between the two families:[1]

Thursday, Jan. 27. Walk with S[helley] about the town seeking lodgings. Call on Mrs. Mason and the pretty Laurette. The weather most exquisitely warm and sunny. Read an Irish pamphlet.
Saturday, Jan. 29. Call at Mrs. Mason's. Laurette calls.
Sunday, Jan. 30. Drink tea at Madame Mason who tells us some very amusing stories of English Prudery. Of a lady who "Mounts her Chastity and rides over us all."
Monday, Jan. 31. Mad Mason and her Children call. Walk with Laurette.
Tuesday, Feb. 1. Mad Mason calls. Walk with Laurette on the Argine [Causeway].
Wednesday, Feb. 2. Mad Mason calls. Walk a little with Laurette.

Thursday, Feb. 3. We dine at Madame Mason's. She talks to us of her sisters Caroline & Lady Diana di Richi.
Friday, Feb. 4. Walk with Laurette on the Argine.
Saturday, Feb. 5. Walk with Laurette and call in Casa Silva. Vaccà calls & says I am scrofulous and I say he is ridiculous. M[ary] and S[helley] drink tea at Casa Silva.
Sunday, Feb. 6. Walk with Laurette on the Argine and the banks of the Arno. Vaccà calls. Drive with Nerina & Laurette on the Lung'Arno after dinner to see the Mascherata. Drink tea in Casa Silva.
Tuesday, Feb. 8. Laurette calls. In the Evening go to the Opera with Laurette, Shelley and Signor Zanetti.
Thursday, Feb. 10. Call in Casa Silva. Ride in the Mascherata with the Children.
Tuesday, Feb. 15. Walk on the Argine with Laurette. This is the last day of the Carnival. Drive on the Lung'Arno with the children Masked.
Friday, Feb. 18. Story of the pretty Laurette. It was necessary to have one of her teeth drawn but her Mamma and *Tatty* could not resolve to give her the pain. She, understanding this, went secretly for the dentist, suffered the operation and then told them of it. This happened this afternoon.
Saturday, Feb. 19. Mrs. M has the power of shutting up her nose so that she need not smell bad odours. Vaccà thinks it is the muscle which prevents the food from going from the mouth to the nose which she closes tight. Madame Vaccà by long practice has acquired also this faculty—so at least she says.
Tuesday, Feb. 22. Walk, with Laurette to the convent of Santa Chiara to pay a visit to Betsy an English nun.
Wednesday, Feb. 23. Walk with Laurette by the Back of Scota's garden outside the Florence Gate. Drink Tea

in Casa Silva. Talk over a Plan of Capuccini for Madame du Plantis. Much laughter.

Sunday, Feb. 27. Walk with L[aurette] in the Cascine. Dine in Casa Silva. Lady Oxford used always to travel with an English doctor in her suite. She said one day to a large party, "Well I do not know what I should have done last night. I was so thirsty, had not Bickerstaff, my doctor, who slept in my room got me a glass of water, I should have perished." When she was at Vienna, she used, on the pretence of delicate health, to make this Bickerstaff carry her to and from her carriage in his arms, and she always danced with him which astonished the Germans who thought it *"très drôle que Miladi dansoit toujours avec son accoucheur."*

Monday, Feb. 28. Call in Casa Silva. N[erin]a ill.

Tuesday, Feb. 29. Call in Casa Silva. N[erina] better. Evening go to an Accademme of Music. Many buffa songs by a Priest.

Wednesday, Mar. 1. Call in Casa Silva. Nerina ill of measles.

Thursday, Mar. 2. Call in Casa Silva. Nerina better. Il Signor Vaccà calls. Walk about with L[aurette]. Call at the Convent of Santa Chiara to see Betsy or Suora Ancilla. Our Caterina is sent there.

Thursday, Mar. 9. Our little Percy has the measles.

Saturday, Mar. 11. Walk with Laurette. In the Evening go to the opera with Laurette and G et la Sua Signora.

Monday, Mar. 13. Call in Casa Silva. L[auret]ta ill.

Wednesday, Mar. 15. Talk with Madame M of the Prusic [*sic*] Acid which kills without pain in a few minutes. Of Jackson in the Irish Rebellion a conspirator who tho' he might have escaped from prison refused because it would have involved the safety of others. He knew he should be condemned, and therefore he swallowed a strong poison. . . .

Sunday, April 19. Call in Casa Silva. Lady M—told Volney how happy she was to see the author of the *Ruins of Empire*. He said Never wish to see an author. Content yourself with his book & be assured it is the best part about him. And the manners of Volney were so rude & rough that she was tempted to say *Ecce signum*.

Tuesday, April 21. Drink tea in Casa Silva. Shelley to Livorno. Mrs. M also told a very droll story. Giunto-tardi a Roman friend of her's came to her one morning & informed that an old priest one of their friends had just lost his mistress and was in extreme distress about it. She was not in very good spirits but as it was a sorrowful errand felt less objection to go. They entered the room, the Giunto-tardi & the Signor Tighe who also accompanied them; they found the old priest shaking in a cold room & holding in his shrivelled hands a little pit of fire. They condoled & he told how grieved he was for the loss of "una fresca donna di sessant' anni." Giunto-tardi was in an agony but when he saw the Signora Contessa hiding her face with both her hands to hide the violence of her laughter & the Signor Tighe give way to an "*éclat de rire*" he could hold no longer to the great surprize of the priest who beheld his polite condolers fail in the very tenderest part of his story. [This episode took place in 1804, while Mrs. Mason was still Lady Mount Cashell.]

Tuesday, April 28. See Tatty who has a very agreeable countenance.

Friday, May 5. Breakfast in Casa Silva. Lesson from Legerino. Account of the *Odd* English at present in Pisa. Walter Savage Landor who will not see a single English person says he is glad his country produces people of worth but he will have nothing to do with them. Shelley

Laurette Tighe

*From drawings by an unknown
artist, about 1830*

Nerina Tighe

"Mrs. Mason," the Dowager
Countess of Mount Cashell
From an Italian colored lithograph

who walks about reading a great quarto Encyclopedia with another volume under his arm. *Tatty* who sets potatoes in pots, & a Mr. Dolby who is rejoicing that he is escaped from England at last although he is 70 some say 80 yrs of age—he is short & thick, goes about with his pockets stuffed out with books, singing, & a pair of spectacles hung by a gold chain round his neck. He is learned & tells every one that he would put on a better coat to visit them in if he had another in the world besides the one he wears.

During the first few months of 1820, the Shelleys saw almost nobody but Mrs. Mason and her family. Claire spent her time studying music and dancing—and visiting the Masons. Mary tended her little boy, read much—and visited the Masons. At Casa Silva there was warmth, wit, good advice, good conversation, and a good library; it took Claire at least four days to arrange the books in order. The talk was advanced and liberal, the reading concerned to some extent with Irish history. The journals of the two young women show that, although Mary received Mrs. Mason's first welcome, Claire gradually became the closer friend. It was Claire who walked out daily with Laurette, who arranged the books, who took the children to the carnival or to the opera. Mary, who was naturally a colder, more reserved woman, had a husband and child. Claire turned for help to Mrs. Mason, her adviser, or, in Claire's words, her "Minerva." They saw less of Tatty, Mr. Tighe, for he loved solitude so much that he appeared seldom in the drawing room, but when he did he impressed all with his courtesy and old-fashioned notions of honor. He was, says Claire, "a most accurate and penetrating judge of human nature; he had lived with the hermit and the sage in their refined solitude; he had lived in the world, and had learned that the man bred in the world and living for it has seldom any heart or conscience."[2]

Of course, Shelley was also a frequent visitor. One can imagine the liberally hot discussions of the Irish republican and the English radical, the flaming zeal of the young poet and the sincere, if disillusioned, liberalism of the woman. Shelley's early impressions of Mrs. Mason, which he wrote to Leigh Hunt, are contained in the introduction to this book. He praised her also in a letter to Hogg dated April 20, 1820. "I have been fortunate enough," he wrote, "to make acquaintance here with a most interesting woman, in whose society we spend a great part of our time. She is married, and has two children; her husband is, what husbands too commonly are, far inferior to her, but not in the proportion of Mrs. Gisborne's. You will have some idea of the sort of person, when I tell you that I am now reading with her the 'Agamemnon' of Aeschylus."[3] But his greatest tribute to her was written in verse. Mrs. Mason was, Shelley told his cousin Thomas Medwin, the source of inspiration of his "Sensitive Plant," the scene of which was laid in her garden.[4] He wrote the poem in March of 1820.

The *Mimosa pudica* (the shy mimosa, or sensitive plant) is an evergreen native to Brazil but widely naturalized in warm countries. Its numerous tiny leaflets are arranged along its stem feather-fashion, and these leaflets when touched will instantly fold up face to face, recoiling from the irritation of the external world. Shelley identified himself with the plant.

His poem—symbolical, mystical, Platonistic, autobiographical—pictures a garden in bloom tended by its mistress. There is a flow of sympathy and love between the flowers of the garden and the Lady, until she dies. Then the foul ravages of death descend upon her and her flowers; the Sensitive Plant is a leafless wreck; mandrakes, toadstools, docks, and darnels rise. Has all this love and beauty died? No.

> That garden sweet, that lady fair,
> And all sweet shapes and odors there,
> In truth have never passed away:
> 'Tis we, 'tis ours, are changed; not they.

Shelley told his cousin that Mrs. Mason was the Lady, "a superior and accomplished woman, and a great resource to him."[5] She too was a sensitive plant, naturalized in a warm country, avoiding for half the years of her life the touch that would make her sensitivity recoil.

Shelley's health showed some improvement in Pisa. As Mrs. Mason had expected, Vaccà, who "could only guess" at the cause of Shelley's pains, guessed that much of the malady was attributable to nervous causes. He exhorted Shelley to abstain from drugs and remedies and physicians, and to leave the healing of his complaint to nature. Warm baths would be likely to do more good than medicine. Besides being a competent physician, Vaccà was a liberal and an atheist, after Shelley's own heart both intellectually and professionally.

It is all very well to diagnose an ailment as being psychosomatic; it is another thing to remove the cause. Few men have had more justification than Shelley to develop nervous disorders. Godwin and his finances were becoming intolerable. Creditors were hounding Shelley himself for old debts. Mary and Claire were bickering, and Claire was growing more and more agitated about Allegra and how she fared with Byron. A little girl, Elena, whom Shelley had adopted in Naples, died. ("My Neapolitan charge is dead," Shelley wrote to the Gisbornes. "It seems as if the destruction that is consuming me were as an atmosphere which wrapt and *in-fected* every thing connected with me.")[6]   Shelley's former servant, Paolo, was attempting to blackmail him. The agony in his side may have been due to a kidney stone, but Shelley had what he called "moral causes" enough.

Tatty, too, had been unwell, confined the whole winter with an attack of rheumatism.   Vaccà ordered him to take the baths at Casciano in May, and Mary Shelley undertook to help him find lodgings.   She wrote to her friend Mrs. Gisborne in Leghorn asking for help.[7]   Tatty wanted a sitting room, a bedroom for himself, and another for his servant, as near as possible to the baths.   The servant went first to secure the lodgings where Tatty was to stay from May 13 to June 14, with one brief visit back to Pisa on June 1 and 2.   Shelley visited him twice there; after each visit he reported to Casa Silva on the progress the invalid was making.

Mary and, particularly, Claire continued their intimacy with Mrs. Mason and her daughters.   Together they walked on the Argine, drove on the Florence or the Lucca road, went to the religious services at the Cathedral on Corpus Domini day.   Claire and Laurette and another friend, Gigia, made excursions such as the one on June 8 when the three spent the day walking about the hills of "this delightful place" Pugnano.   "A better day than most days and good reason for it, though Shelley is not well," Mary wrote in her journal.   Then she added, "Claire away at Pugnano."   On the last day of May, Miss Mathilda Field, the expected English schoolteacher, arrived to be the houseguest and companion of Mrs. Mason.[8]

On June 15 Shelley took his household to Leghorn, where they remained until August 5.   The reason for the move was that Shelley wished to be near his lawyer, Federico del Rosso, whom he had engaged to silence his former servant, Paolo Foggi, the "superlative rascal" who in trying to blackmail him was spreading scandalous stories. The stories included the charge that Shelley's Neapolitan ward, Elena, was the daughter of Shelley and Claire. With information now available, the charge can easily be proved false;[9] a more likely bit of gossip might be that the child was the daughter of Shelley and Élise, the Swiss governess, who was by this time the wife of Paolo.[10]

The visiting between the families was not entirely discontinued, for Pisa is only a few miles from Leghorn. On July 18 Claire left for Casa Silva where she stayed until the twentieth, when she and Tatty, Mrs. Mason, and Miss Field set out at five in the morning for Leghorn. They arrived at seven-thirty, and spent the day with the Shelleys. Shelley took Claire's place on the return to Pisa at six that evening.

On July 30 Shelley wrote to Mary from Casa Silva to tell her that he had rented a pleasant and spacious house, Casa Prinni, at the Baths of Pisa for three months. In the same letter he told her that Tatty was planning a journey to England to secure his property in the event of a revolution, for the echoes of the English political clamor that reached Pisa produced there mixed emotions of liberal hope of revolution and financial fear of ruin. "Money will be delayed," Shelley wrote, "and the exchange reduced very low, and my annuity and Mrs. Masons on account of their being *money* will be in some danger, but land is quite safe. Besides it will not be so rapid. Let us hope we shall have a Reform. Tatty will be lulled into a security while the slow progress of things is still flowing on after this affair of the Queen may appear to be blown over."[11] (Poor Queen Caroline, wife of George IV, was defending herself against charges, one of which was that she had been observed under a tarpaulin on the deck of a ship in the Bay of Naples supine beneath an Italian servant prone.) Mrs. Mason was unhappy at the prospect of Tatty's going to England, though she felt it necessary that he go some time to settle his affairs.

Back in Ireland Tatty's friends were pleased that they might soon see him again. His friend and agent, Charles Hamilton, kept him informed of conditions in Ireland. When George IV visited Dublin the next April, Hamilton wrote, "We have been literally in a fever for the last month since the arrival of His Majesty in Ireland: Dublin was as full as it used to be before the union with the addition to our own great folks of numbers of English & foreigners. The King seems to have been happily pleased with his reception which indeed was beyond anything he could have expected considering the manner in which he has been treated in England but here we don't trouble ourselves about the Amours of Kings or Queens nor do we much care who are his Majestys ministers well knowing that it cannot make much difference to us and that one & all they will take as much from us & give us as little as they can, but an Irishman & particularly a Catholic is naturally loyal & a kind word or two would do more in this country than the whole standing army could do in England. The King knows the point in which to trust Paddy and the day of his public entry when he attempted to address the people but could not be heard by one hundredth part of them, he took a large shamrock from his hat & placed it in his bosom which pleased his audience better than if he had spoken for an hour."[12] But Tatty did not have to go to England after all; at least there is no record, even on his passport, of a trip back home.

Instead we find continued record of trips to the Shelleys at Casa Prinni or by the Shelleys and Claire to Casa

Silva. On one such visit, when Mrs. Mason, the children, and Miss Field were visiting at the Baths, Shelley read his "Ode to Liberty" to the ladies accompanied by the loud gruntings of innumerable pigs brought for sale to the fair of St. Bartholomew, for it was August 24. The gruntings reminded the party of the chorus of frogs in Aristophanes, and Shelley was inspired to write his *Swellfoot the Tyrant* in which, against a background of grunting pigs as a chorus, the King's ministers seek to ruin the Queen by pouring over her head the contents of a green bag full of perjured testimony. The volume was suppressed.

Mrs. Mason had long been aware of a troublesome circumstance in the Shelley household which ought to have been apparent to anybody less impractical than the poet. One cause of the pain in Shelley's side was the thorn in Mary's, and that thorn was Claire, or the presence of Claire. Shelley liked and protected her with an affection that was not likely to reduce the antipathy between the two women. Mary wrote spiteful remarks in her journal, and Claire on one occasion was moved to verse. "Heigh-ho!" she wrote in *her* journal, "the Claire and the Ma Find something to fight about every day."[13] Furthermore, the presence of Claire in the household gave the gossips fuel, as even the blackmailer Paolo could well perceive. Claire had no alternative but to live with the Shelleys until Mrs. Mason used her good offices. Mrs. Mason was, as we have seen, "unacquainted" in Florence; but she had connections, for in the fall she arranged that Claire was to go to the house of Professor Boiti,[14] where she could live while she took pupils in English. Boiti, who was one of the court physicians to the Grand Duke of Tuscany, lived opposite the Pitti Palace, in the neighborhood to be made famous in literary history by the residence of the Brownings. On October 20, 1820, the faithful Shelley accompanied Claire from Pisa to Florence and left her there. Claire wrote in her journal, "Whoever does a benefit to another buys so much envy, malice, hatred and all uncharitableness from him."[15] Whatever could have suggested the thought?

Immediately the atmosphere in the Shelley household cleared: Mrs. Mason had been right. But Claire was not happy in Florence. Within a week she was melancholy and disconsolate, so that even her friends Signor and Signora Tantini took notice, imputing her feelings to the weather. "You must indeed be very uncomfortable for it to become visible to them," Shelley wrote to her.[16] His liberty-loving instinct was that Claire should return to Pisa at once—to begin again, inevitably, the merry-go-round of bickering—but he did not want Claire to offend Mrs. Mason. Mrs. Mason, who was less of a fanatic for "liberty" than was Shelley, remained firm. Claire should stay. A note of pique appeared in Shelley's letter: "I have seen little lately of Mrs. M.," he told Claire, "nor when one sees her is it easy to nail her attention to what you wish to say, unless you make a direct demand, which in the present case I can hardly do."[17] The outcome was that Claire remained with the Boitis.

Claire continued unhappy and homesick in Florence, and Shelley encouraged her to leave, fraught as her position in Florence was with consequences to her health and spirits that he could not endure to think of. He and Mrs. Mason had long discussions on the subject, but she remained adamant that Claire should not rejoin the Shelley household. Claire's agreement was to spend a trial-month with the Boitis before deciding on any future commitment. If she still found the place unbearable, Mrs. Mason would give her a letter to the Princess Montemiletto, who might take Claire under her protection in Florence. "The only consideration to make you hesitate," Shelley wrote to Claire, "*is* how far such a step [returning to Pisa] would offend Mrs. Mason—that is, how far it would affect any future aid you might derive from her. Poor Mrs. M. is now very ill, slowly convalescing from a dangerous colic; she cannot bear the light, or the air, or the least motion. You may judge, she is [in] no state to permit me to agitate this question. Before her illness, when I talked to her, she seemed to think it weak and unreasonable in you, not to bear all this solitude and inconvenience in the hope of some change, or something that she could do or would do. She opposed strongly the idea of your return; and it was on that occasion that she spoke of the Princess Montemiletto; which introduction, if it could be carried into effect, would certainly place you in a situation to require no other. But as she has not seen or heard from the Princess for 16 years, we cannot be sure of the reception her recommendation would meet. . . . My advice therefore is, that you take a place in the Diligence and return here instantly, without offending or alarming the Boitis. You cannot hesitate without making yourself liable for an engagement of three additional months, and I am persuaded that Mrs. Mason is too reasonable and too good not to feel that this step is completely justifiable. . . ."[18] Claire arrived in Pisa on November 21, the day after her month with the Boitis was over.

Again Claire resumed her daily visits to Casa Silva, recorded the visits in her journal, and occasionally wrote down some statement that Mrs. Mason had made, such as that on December 14: "One of Madame M's rules, to consider a prejudiced person as one labouring under a serious illness." The Shelleys depended less now on Mrs. Mason for society, because they had made friends with a

motley group of Pisans: Francesco Pacchiano, known as
"Il Diavolo," professor, canon, poet, rogue; the *improvvisatore* Tommaso Sgricci; Prince Alexander Mavrocordato,
a Greek patriot; and Emilia Viviani, a beautiful nineteen-
year-old Italian girl whose parents had imprisoned her in
a convent awaiting her marriage.   Mrs. Mason seems to
have thought the imprisonment less monstrous than did
Shelley.   Claire dined at Casa Silva on December 22 and
the next day returned to the Boitis in Florence, taking with
her Mrs. Mason's letter to the Princess Montemiletto.

Claire's life in Florence was now less disconsolate, even
gay.   The Boitis were kind to her, and her account of the
festivities during Carnival shows that she was not unhappy.   Yet always, always at the back of her mind was
the thought of her daughter Allegra, whom Byron would
not allow her to see.   His attitude toward Claire had run
full circle.   During their brief period of love-making
when Allegra was conceived, Claire (some think) inspired him to write what may be his best love poem:

> There be none of Beauty's daughters
>   With a magic like thee;
> And like music on the waters
>   Is thy sweet voice to me.

Only a few weeks after composing these lines, he found
the sweet voice tiresome; still later he wrote in exaspera-
tion, "To express it delicately, I think Madame Clare is
a damn bitch."[19]   The thought of seeing her was enough
to put him into a rage.

Mrs. Hoppner, wife of the British Consul at Venice,
had written Claire alarming news about the debauched
life that Byron led there and the impropriety of raising a
child in his household.   Élise, the child's governess, told
tales that would stagger Aphrodite.   "The nurse I men-

tioned wrote to me every week to state how the Child was," Claire wrote to Trelawny fifty years after the event. "About three months afterwards I got a letter from her in which she told me that the day before, Lord Byron had been in the nursery and sat some time observing Allegrina at play. Of a sudden he said to the nurse, 'She will grow up a very pretty woman and then I will take her for my mistress.' Élise was shocked and said, 'I suppose My Lord you are joking, but even as a joke, it is a very improper one.' He answered he was not joking at all. 'I'll do it.' She seemed still further shocked. He then said—'I can very well do it—she is no child of mine. She is Mr. Shelley's child.' Next day she wrote me what had passed. On reading her letter I felt extreme indignation and extreme alarm. For the first time there rushed into my mind the idea that he was a most wicked man. I shewed Élise's letter to Lady M[ount Cashell] and asked her advice—and she was of opinion I must go to Venice directly, withdraw Allegra from his protection and drop all intercourse with him. She promised to give me the means to emigrate with my Child to Australia—and there I would set up a school and earn our breads and far from the wicked lead a peaceful life."[20] This shocking charge need not be credited: Élise was something of a trouble-maker, and Claire was an unreliable reporter of fact, even when she had not brooded on her wrongs for fifty years.

"I must tell you," Claire continued, "Lady M on two accounts had ever had a bad opinion of Lord Byron; first from his writings she thought them the greater part of them calculated to demoralize rather than elevate. Everywhere he sneers at Truth, Virtue, Justice, Benevolence and considers them as Utopias. He describes fatal impulses in Love, fatal impulses in Hatred with great strength and idealized them by poetry as far as ugly deformed things can be idealized, and it was this constant inclination in him to treat only painful subjects which made her distrust him. She constantly said the soul becomes like what it contemplates and no man who invariably recreates his intellect with subjects full of vicious disorder can be anything but a bad man. His writings gave her the impression that Fury was his wisdom, revenge his religion."[21]

Hardly had the gaiety of Carnival given way to the austerity of Lent when Claire received news that tormented her for the rest of her life. Byron had placed Allegra in a Capuchin convent at Bagnacavallo. He was now living in Ravenna with his "last attachment," the Contessa Teresa Guiccioli, married daughter of an Italian nobleman. Claire imagined that Allegra was living a life of severe asceticism, unfed and unloved, in a cold convent, surrounded by malaria-infested marshes. Byron, who wanted his daughter to become a Catholic and live on the Continent, would have no daughter of his exposed to Shelley's atheism and vegetarianism. Besides, he believed the blackmail charges that Shelley and Claire had a daughter which they had placed in a foundling hospital.

Claire's conscious and subconscious minds turned naturally to Casa Silva for help. On April 21, 1821, she wrote in her journal, "I dreamed this night that Tatty had been to Bagnacavallo and had returned bringing Allegra to me. He said Mr. Hobhouse was at Ravenna but had declined interfering. A Miss O'Neile there had threatened Albè [Byron] who then allowed Allegra to come on a visit to me. I rejoiced [and] said to S[helley] now she shall never go back again." On June 6, she recorded another dream: "Towards Wednesday morning I had a most distressing dream—that I received a letter which said that Allegra was ill and not likely to live. The dreadful grief I felt made awaking appear to me the most delightful sensation of ease in the world. Just so, I think, must the wearied soul feel when it finds itself in Paradise, released from the trembling anguish of the world."

Shelley and Mary tried to reassure her that Allegra was well protected and well cared for in the convent. "So far have I been from neglecting you in my thoughts," he wrote to Claire on April 29, "that I have lately had with Mrs. Mason long and serious conversations respecting your situation and prospects; conversations too long, too important, and embracing too various a complication of views to detail in a letter. You can perhaps guess at some of them."[22] One project discussed involved Claire's setting up a school under the patronage of Mrs. Mason. "But the idea of a school, especially under Miss [sic] Mason's protection, I confess appeared very plausible to me," he wrote Claire. "I should be glad, in case of transmigration, to leave you under such powerful and such sure protection as her's: it would be one subject less for regret, to me, if I could consider—my death—as no immediate misfortune to you; as in this case it would not."[23]

In August, without letting Claire know, Shelley made a trip to Ravenna to see Lord Byron and then to Bagnacavallo to see Allegra. Byron was planning to leave Ravenna, perhaps for Pisa. He wanted especially to find a place where there were no English, and Shelley's apprehension was that he might settle near Claire. "Gunpowder and fire ought to be kept at a respectable distance from each other," he wrote to Mary.[24] When he visited Allegra, he found her grown tall, slight, delicate, pale. Before he left, Byron's four-year-old daughter rang the convent assembly bell which almost brought scampering nuns to their posts. Nobody scolded her.

While Shelley was still at Ravenna, Byron decided definitely upon Pisa and commissioned Shelley to find him a sufficiently luxurious palace there. The Shelleys themselves considered the possibility of going elsewhere, perhaps to Florence. There were many arguments in favor of remaining: "Our roots never struck so deeply as at Pisa, and the transplanted tree flourishes not," he wrote to Mary. "People who lead the lives which we led until last winter, are like a family of Wahabee Arabs, pitching their tent in the midst of London."[25]   On the other hand, Pisa was not entirely satisfactory: "The Masons are there," he wrote, "and as far as solid affairs are concerned are my friends. I allow this is an argument for Florence. Mrs. Mason's perverseness is very annoying to me especially as Mr. Tighe is seriously my friend and this circumstance makes me averse from that intimate continuation of intercourse which, once having begun, I can no longer avoid."[26]   How Mrs. Mason was perverse we can only guess, but a good guess is that her common sense on the subject of Claire was deaf to the voice of Shelley's ethereal reason. Shelley, the knight, was ready to rescue any high-born maiden from a palace tower. Mrs. Mason, worldly wise, refused to grant that an independent Claire in Florence was imprisoned in a tower at all and insisted that she should not by any means live with the Shelleys. After all considerations, the Shelleys decided to remain in Pisa.

But what was to become of Allegra? Shelley had almost persuaded Byron to take her with him. However, Byron's house was manifestly unfit for the education of a child, even though, under the influence of La Guiccioli, it was no longer a "theater of excess." "Is there any family, any English or Swiss establishment, any refuge in short except the convent of St. Anna where Allegra

might be placed?" Shelley asked Mary. "Do you think
Mrs. Mason could be prevailed on to *propose* to take
charge of her? I fear not. Think of this against I
come."[27] He also proposed to Byron a respectable private
family, but Allegra had to remain in the convent when
Byron established himself, his worldly goods, his servants,
and his animals* in the Palazzo Lanfranchi in Pisa, which
Shelley rented for him from Dr. Vaccà.[28]

The pressing problem was to get Claire back to
Florence before Byron arrived in Pisa. When the coach
in which she was traveling Florence-ward neared Empoli,
the driver pulled off to the side of the road to allow safe
passage to the carriage of an English lord traveling with
his company in the opposite direction.

With the arrival of Lord Byron on November 1,
things in sleepy Pisa began to pick up. There were a few
scenes, a few servant stabbings, a street fight with an
Italian dragoon. The Tuscan authorities made life difficult for the politically minded Gambas, Teresa Guiccioli's
father and brother, who accompanied Byron. Groups of
English would gather outside Byron's magnificent residence to catch a glimpse of him leaving or entering. Mrs.
Mason was not among them, nor did she ever meet him.
He went his dramatic way, and she thrived in her tran-
quility.

On January 14, 1822, Byron, Shelley, and their Pisan
circle were joined by Edward Trelawny, a young, six-foot,
dark, handsome, Arab-like, English adventurer. Restless
and picturesque, he was drawn to Pisa because Shelley was
there; though he had never met the poet, he knew and
admired his poetry. At first the Shelleys did not know
what to make of him, but they saw that he was honest,

* Shelley counted ten horses, eight enormous dogs, three monkeys, five
cats, an eagle, a crow, and a falcon. He had overlooked five peacocks,
two guinea hens, and an Egyptian crane.

clever, and eloquent in recounting his adventures. One ingredient of his personality that attracted him to the sea-loving Shelley was that he had been a sailor and knew more about the sea and sailing than any other member of the Pisan circle. When the circle proposed to present Shakespeare's *Othello*, Trelawny was inevitably chosen to play the noble Moor. In real life he was a sort of Othello who could win a maid on his own merits or on the merits of his traveler's history. Byron was to play Iago.

Back in Florence, Claire Clairmont had fallen into evil company, to wit, Élise, Allegra's governess. Élise has been with good cause accused of slandering Claire, and now, in reverse, she was slandering Byron. Naturally Claire was alarmed at what she heard and wrote to Byron on February 18, pleading for an opportunity to see her daughter before she left Italy. Mrs. Mason had advised Claire to join her brother Charles in Vienna, and to that end Claire had been diligently and successfully studying German and German literature. "I shall shortly leave Italy for a new country," she wrote to Byron, "to enter upon a disagreeable and precarious course of life; I yield in this not to my own wishes, but to the advice of a friend whose head is wiser than mine. I leave my friends with regret, but indeed I cannot go without having first seen and embraced Allegra. Do not, I entreat you, refuse me this little, but only, consolation."[29] Byron was unmoved, and Claire in some panic went to Pisa to consult with Mrs. Mason and Shelley. Years later Claire wrote that Tatty, after a secret trip to Bagnacavallo, had reported frightful things about the cold, damp, austere convent; but Tatty's visit may have grown entirely out of the dream Claire had on April 21—his passport records no such trip.

Shelley then went to Byron to present an appeal on Claire's behalf. He told Mrs. Mason of his interview with Byron, and Betsy Parker wrote the details to Claire. One might well challenge the credibility of Betsy's letter, which exists only in a copy made by Claire. Why did not Claire preserve the original? Why is reference made to Lady Mount Cashell rather than to Mrs. Mason? At any rate, the letter says that Shelley called in the evening at Casa Silva to discuss his interview with Byron. Mrs. Mason, Tatty, and Betsy were present.

"I never saw him [Shelley] in a passion before," Betsy wrote, "last night, however, he was downright, positively angry. . . . Mr. Shelley declared to Lady Mount-cashell that he could with pleasure have knocked Lord Byron down; for when he mentioned that you were half-distracted with alarm about the child's health, and also that you were yourself in very declining health, he saw a gleam of malicious satisfaction pass over Lord Byron's countenance. 'I saw his look,' Mr. Shelley said; 'I understood its meaning; I despised him, and I came away.' These were his own epigrammatic words. Afterwards he said, 'It is foolish of me to be angry with him; he can no more help being what he is than yonder door can help being a door.' Mr. Tighe then said, 'You are quite wrong in your fatalism. If I were to horsewhip that door, it would still remain a door; but if Lord Byron were well horsewhipped, my opinion is he would become as humane as he is now inhumane. It is the feeble character or the subserviency of his friends that makes him the insolent tyrant that he is!' This observation Mr. Shelley repelled; he said others were free, of course, to use the law of coercion; he disapproved it, and the only law that should ever govern his conduct should be the law of love. The discussion appeared to be getting warm, these two think so differently; therefore Lady Mountcashell carried Mr. Shelley off to read Euripides, and the subject dropped."[30]

Claire, brooding in her despair, devised a plan that was as reckless and dangerous as could be. It would involve Shelley, and perhaps Tatty, in forging a letter, taking it to the convent at Bagnacavallo, and kidnapping Allegra. She would then have her daughter to herself hidden away from Lord Byron. Both Shelley and Mary wrote in great alarm dissuading Claire from her mad design.[31] Byron was a wealthy man, they wrote, ruthless and implacable. He would track them down aided by his wealth and position, and certainly Shelley's involvement could result only in a duel. Byron would very likely be obliged to go to England within a year to settle his property there, and with him removed from the scene the chances of rescuing Allegra would be greater. Claire's plan was concocted in the spring of 1822, and Mary used a curious argument to dissuade her. "No spring has passed for us without some piece of ill luck," she wrote, and then listed seven tragedies that had occurred in the seven springs that she and Shelley had been together.[32] Wait till autumn. One wonders what would have happened had Claire appealed not to Shelley but to Trelawny.

When Trelawny did meet Claire, he was immediately attracted to her. She—exotic, distractingly pretty, and in trouble—had all the ingredients that would appeal to his susceptibilities. Afterwards, when he was proposing that she be his wife or mistress or at least accept money from him, he said, "you have one faithful bosom—(unchangeable)—that if his lot is equally wretched—or otherwise—will receive you and press you to his bosom with the same undiminished ardor he did when he first pressed you there."[33] Again he said, "Friendship and love has by being mutual and acknowledged given me the first and

strongest power over you."[34]   And still later he said,
"our friendship had a violent commencement and then,
lured by fancy or driven by fate, we wandered by different paths."[35]   What would have been the result had
she accepted him?

On April 15 Claire arrived in Pisa for a brief visit with
the Shelleys. Four days later Allegra died at Bagnacavallo, at the age of five years and three months. Claire
had known nothing of her child's illness, but her dreams
had been prophetic: Allegra had been suffering with
typhus fever for weeks. All agreed that under no circumstances should the news be broken to Claire while
she was near Byron. On April 26 the Shelleys rented the
Villa Magni on the very edge of the sea in the Bay of
Spezia north of Pisa. Two or three times Claire attempted
to return to Florence, but the Shelleys persuaded her to
stay. On May 2, the day after Jane and Edward Williams, good friends, were installed with the Shelleys for
the summer, Claire announced definitely that she would
leave the crowded house. The Shelleys and Williams
were discussing how best to break the news to her when
she walked into the room and knew at once by their faces
what had happened. Shelley told her.

Her first reaction was one of shock, and Shelley
thought she would lose her reason. But she soon achieved
a strange, mournful calm, as if relieved that fate no longer
had a weapon to hold over her to wring her heart with
wounds that neither kill nor heal. A remorseful Byron
granted Claire's requests for a miniature of Allegra and
a lock of her hair. Mrs. Mason's man of business, Pompeo
Biondi, went to Bagnacavallo to make the funeral arrangements,[36] and Mrs. Mason wrote to Claire attempting to
console her, pointing out that had Allegra lived she would
have been a constant source of misery and that Claire's

life would be more tranquil in the future. Claire remained at Casa Magni for almost three weeks.

Casa Magni had other worries: Mary was pregnant, and Mrs. Mason was protecting her against the "summit and crown of her misfortune" that spring, the bad news that her father had lost a lawsuit and was being evicted. "I send you in return for Godwin's letter one still worse," Mrs. Mason wrote to Shelley, "because I think it has more the appearance of truth. I was desired to convey it to Mary, but that I should not think right. At the same time, I don't well know how you can conceal all this affair from her; they really seem to want assistance at present, for their being turned out of the house is a serious evil. . . .

"Mary ought to know what is said of the novel [Mary's novel *Valperga* which she had sent to her father for publication], and how can she know that without all the rest? You will contrive what is best. In the part of the letter which I do send, she [Mrs. Godwin] adds, that at this moment Mr. Godwin does not offer the novel to any bookseller, lest his actual situation might make it be supposed that it would be sold cheap. Mrs. Godwin also wishes to correspond directly with Mrs. Shelley, but this I shall not permit; she says Godwin's health is much the worse for all this affair.

"I was astonished at seeing Clare walk in on Tuesday evening, and I have not a spare bed now in the house, the children having outgrown theirs, and been obliged to occupy that which I had formerly; she proposed going to an inn, but preferred sleeping on a sofa, where I made her as comfortable as I could, which is but little so; however, she is satisfied. I rejoice to see that she has not suffered so much as you expected, and understand now her former feelings better than at first. When there is nothing to hope or fear, it is natural to be calm. I wish she had some determined project, but her plans seem as unsettled as ever, and she does not see half the reasons for separating herself from your society that really exist. I regret to perceive her great repugnance to Paris, which I believe to be the place best adapted to her. If she had but the temptation of good letters of introduction—but I have no means of obtaining them for her—she intends, I believe, to go to Florence to-morrow, and to return to your habitation in a week, but talks of not staying the whole summer.

"I regret the loss of Mary's good health and spirits, but hope it is only the consequence of her present situation, and therefore merely temporary, but I dread Clare's being in the same house for a month or two, and wish the Williams' were a half a mile from you. I must write a few lines to Mary, but will say nothing of having heard from Mrs. Godwin; you will tell her what you think right, but you know my opinion, that things which cannot be concealed, are better told at once. I should suppose a bankruptcy would be best, but the Godwins do not seem to think so. If all the world valued obscure tranquillity as much as I do, it would be a happier, though possibly much duller, world than it is, but the loss of wealth is quite an epidemic disease in England. . . ."[37]

On May 12 one of Shelley's dreams materialized. As he and Williams were walking on the terrace of Casa Magni after dinner, they spotted a strange sail entering the Bay of Spezia. It was the *Don Juan*, Shelley's long-awaited boat, a "perfect little ship" twenty-four feet by eight, with a four-foot draught. Daily Shelley and Williams went sailing, passing other craft in the bay "as a comet might pass the dullest planet," in spite of the casual seamanship of Shelley, who liked to read and steer at the same time. "You will do nothing with Shelley," Trelawny told Williams, "until you heave his books and papers overboard, sheer the wisps of hair that hang over his eyes; and plunge his arms up to the elbows in a tar-bucket."[38]   Shelley never knew such joy. His health had improved beyond expectation. "My only regret," he said, "is that the summer must ever pass. . . ."[39]

Yet this surface joy of Shelley's concealed a serious disturbance which manifested itself in visions. Once while pacing on the terrace of Casa Magni with Williams, he saw a naked child rise suddenly from the sea and clap its hands in joy. "There it is again—There!" he cried. He was sure it was Allegra, and Williams had difficulty in convincing him that he had not witnessed reality. Once he met his own figure walking on the terrace, and the figure demanded of him, *"Siete contento?"*   Another time he had dreams or visions that the sea was flooding the house and that he was strangling Mary. On the morning of June 16, Mary, who had been alarmingly unwell for over a week, suffered a miscarriage and nearly lost her life.

Two days later Shelley wrote to Trelawny, "should you meet with any scientific person, capable of preparing the *Prussic Acid, or essential oil of bitter almonds,* I should regard it as a great kindness if you could procure me a small quantity. . . .   I need not tell you I have no intention of suicide at present, but I confess it would be a comfort to me to hold in my possession that golden key to the chamber of perpetual rest."[40]   For over two years he had remembered the conversation in Casa Silva when Mrs. Mason had talked about the Prussic Acid which kills without pain in a few minutes.

The next day word came that Leigh Hunt had arrived in Genoa accompanied by his wife and six children. Shelley's plan had been that Hunt should come from England to Pisa and with Byron edit a new magazine, *The Liberal.* Now he had arrived. The Hunts sailed to Leghorn, and Shelley took his new boat there to meet them and to conduct them thence overland to Pisa. On Sunday, July 7, after having established the Hunts on the ground floor of Byron's palace, Shelley called on Mrs. Mason before returning to Leghorn, whence he and Williams were to sail the *Don Juan* back to Casa Magni on Monday. Sunburnt and light hearted, he seemed in excellent health, and Mrs. Mason had never seen him look happier than he did as he left her house.

On Monday night she had two nightmares. She was somewhere, she didn't know where, when Shelley came to her pale and melancholy. "You look ill," she said to him. "You are tired; sit down and eat."

"No," he replied, "I shall never eat more; I have not a soldo left in the world."

"Nonsense," she said, "this is no inn, you need not pay."

"Perhaps," he answered, "it is the worse for that."

Then she awoke, and went to sleep again only to dream that Shelley's son, Percy Florence, was dead. She awoke crying bitterly, and said to herself, "Why, if the little boy should die, I should not feel it in this manner."

She was so moved by these dreams that she mentioned them to her servant in the morning and hoped that all was well with the Shelleys. It was not until a few days later that she learned that Shelley had been drowned on the Monday of her dreams.[41]

On July 18 his body was washed ashore.

CHAPTER **10.**

THE STORY OF THE cremation of Shelley's body has often been told, but never better than by Trelawny. He first had an iron furnace made and then equipped himself with fuel, oil, wine, salt, and frankincense in order to carry out the cremation ritual of the ancient Greeks, whom Shelley had loved. On the morning of August 16, the body was removed from its temporary burial place by the sea and placed in the furnace. As the dry and resinous pine wood blazed, Trelawny, who had been joined by Byron and Leigh Hunt, threw salt and frankincense, oil and wine on the flames. Slowly the body turned to ashes, but the heart remained entire. On impulse, Trelawny thrust his naked hand into the fire and snatched out the heart. Vaccà, when he saw it later, thought that it was unusually small. The ashes were buried in the Protestant Cemetery in Rome near the body of Shelley's son William.

Mrs. Mason received some criticism that seems unfair. Godwin thought her "peculiarly cruel"[1] because she had not sent him the bad news of Shelley's death, and Mary criticized her for being cold. "Of my friends I have only Mrs. Mason to mention," wrote Mary to Mrs. Gisborne; "her coldness has stung me; yet she felt his loss keenly, and would be very glad to serve me; but it is not cold

offers of service one wants. . . ."[2] Actually, Mrs. Mason's
"coldness" will seem to most people warmth. But Mary
was suffering indescribable grief, and people under a strain
will say things in private that they do not really mean.

One by one the circle left Pisa. On September 11
Mary went to Genoa. Mrs. Mason thought that Mary
should go at once to England in order to make arrangements with Sir Timothy Shelley for the support of herself
and her son, but Lord Byron advised her to stay and
promised that he would help finance her. On September
20 Claire left Italy for Vienna. Mrs. Mason had long
been advising her to go there, where she would be under
the protection of her brother Charles and where she could
easily find employment as a teacher of English. "I am to
begin my journey to Vienna on Monday," she wrote to
Mary. "Mrs. Mason will make me go, and the consequence is that it will be double as much, as I am to go
alone. Imagine all the lonely inns, the weary long miles,
if I do. Observe, whatever befalls in life, the heaviest
part, the very dregs of the misfortune fall on me. . . .
But I believe my Minerva is right, for I might wait to all
eternity for a party."[3] Mrs. Mason advised her to notice
the scenery on the way, to employ the healing power of
nature, but Claire found it impossible. "I tried the whole
journey to follow your advice," she wrote, "and admire
the scenery—dearest Lady it was all in vain. I saw not
mountains or vallies, woods or rushing streams, Mrs. K.
admired them, so I suppose they were there. I only saw
my lost darling. . . ."[4]

When Mary and her son moved into lodgings in
Genoa, she discovered that the bitter English residents
there would not receive her.[5] Trelawny later advised her
not to go to England to "encounter poverty and bitter
retrospections" but to remain in Italy where he would

share his income with her.[6]   The little money she had
would go farther in Italy, and she could write her novels
and articles for *The Liberal* just as well in Genoa.   After
he had advised her not to live alone, she engaged two
villas in nearby Albaro, one for herself and the Hunts,
the other for Byron and the Gambas.   There the two
households worked on the new magazine, the first issue of
which was a great success because it contained Byron's
libelous poem, *The Vision of Judgment.*

Living with the Hunts was a trial: the six children
were not to be corrected, in Hunt's view, "until such time
as they were of an age to be reasoned with," even though
they were, in Byron's view, "dirtier and more mischievous
than Yahoos."   Moreover, Mrs. Hunt, who expected to
produce a seventh child in June, could justify her wretched
housekeeping by being dangerously ill.   Mrs. Mason's
letters to Mary are full of sound advice on how to deal
with Mrs. Hunt's night sweats and loss of appetite.   After
advising against taking any sort of internal remedy except
such as contained nourishment, she added, "I mention all
these things because both as an *invalid* & as a *Physician*
I have had experience of their advantages; & people who
are not so *thoroughly English* as to think all remedies
must come from the apothecary & be manufactured into the
delightful forms of pills, draughts, powder &c. &c. before
they can be useful, may not perhaps despise those ordinary
matters which I recommend."[7]

She also sent Mary a little book which she had written
for Nerina (not yet eight).   This was perhaps her *Stories
for Little Boys and Girls, in Words of One Syllable,* by
the Author of the *Stories of Old Daniel.*   "I am glad you
like the book dedicated to N[erina] & her little friends,"
she wrote.   "I hope it will amuse Percy one of these days.
It is a long time since I have heard from Mrs. G[odwin]

& I do not know how it *sells*. [The book was one of God-win's French and English Juvenile School Library series.] I should not think *well*, as it contains neither *vulgar gentilities* nor *religious cant*."[8]   Mary, in turn, sent Mrs. Mason a sensitive plant,[9] an appropriate gift in honor of Shelley, and Laurette looked forward to tending it with pleasure.   There should be a sensitive plant at Casa Silva.

Mary's sorrows could be diminished if her father-in-law, Sir Timothy Shelley, would make an allowance for her and his grandson, but Sir Timothy was as crotchety as he was wealthy and refused to help the woman whom he suspected of having estranged his son's mind "from the respect due to Lady S[helley] & himself."[10]   If Mary would take Percy to England and place him in the care of a person approved by Sir Timothy, then he would provide for the boy.   But Mary could not live ten days without her son and preferred to support the two of them as best she could by her writings.   Mrs. Mason could hardly believe the news.   If Mary went to England, she thought, the old gentleman would be shamed into contributing to the support of his son's widow.

Claire, too, was having difficulty.   A few weeks after her arrival in Vienna, she and her brother Charles were in trouble with Metternich's police.   An anonymous informer had written the police to report that Charles was the son of William Godwin and Mary Wollstonecraft, radical atheists, as well as the friend of Shelley and Byron, who were no better.   He and Claire were ordered to leave Vienna within five days, but his influential friends were able to have the period of grace extended to four weeks.   Mrs. Mason was distraught when she wrote to Mary: "Charles thinks her connexion with the name of S[helley] may be the occasion, but I am inclined to another name still better known [Lord Byron's, of course] as more likely to be the cause, & for this I have two or three reasons—you may be sure I did not hint this to her & it does not appear to have entered her head—but you may imagine what a state they must be in with their very restricted & uncertain means of support."[11] Everything had looked so promising until the informer had presented his twisted information; now she was ill and ordered to leave. If she could last until spring, she thought, she would like to go and bathe in the sea like a mermaid.

Mrs. Mason attempted to help by interceding with Lord Byron, whom she had never met. Without advising anybody, especially Tatty, who thought all such action a kind of insanity (and Mrs. Mason wasn't quite sure that he was not right), she wrote to Byron on Claire's behalf. The letter is dated "Pisa, December 28 [1822]."

"Your Lordship will think it strange to receive a letter from me—not more so than I do to write it—but after many months of reflection on the subject, I am convinced that it is only rendering justice to the extraordinary powers of mind & noble sentiments displayed in some of the finest compositions extant, to suppose that if any person of humane and honest feelings were simply to lay before you a few facts, it could not be in vain. The Mother of a Being once dear to your heart, is now destitute of the means of subsistence; chiefly in consequence of the unfortunate circumstance which permits the tongue of malice to join her humble name with one of high celebrity—for without that fatal obstacle, she is as capable of earning her bread as thousands who exist in happy obscurity. Your Lordship intended to make a provision for the Child, of which a small part would redeem your honour, by giving sufficient independence to the Mother, whose claim on you is undeniable. I am aware that you have had cause of irritation; but surely a mind like yours must soon forget such offences; and I am certain that you will never more be troubled on account of that Individual, unless she comes to some dreadful end through the want of that which you would scarcely miss. Though your Lordship does not know me, yet I *feel* that you will give credit to my *solemn assertion*, that I have never been applied to by any person, directly or indirectly, to address you on this subject. I am partly urged by motives of benevolence & partly by respect for genius to remind you of what your various occupations may have driven from your memory: and I shall offer no apology for thinking so well of your heart as to suppose that my letter cannot offend. If the words which I have written do not produce any effect, I shall at least feel no shame for having penned them; & if they do, I shall be rejoiced to find that I have not mistaken your Lordship's character, but may continue without compunction, / Your very sincere Admirer / M. Mason.

"P.S. As no person in the world knows of my writing this letter, whether you attend to it or whether you disregard it, the whole transaction may remain for ever a secret between your Lordship & me."[12]

But Byron was not one to keep a secret. He replied to Mrs. Mason in a nine-page sneering letter giving reasons for refusing his slightest aid to Claire, and he told the whole story to Mary, apparently suspecting that Claire had solicited the intercession. Mrs. Mason did not regret her "Quixotic folly," although she was disillusioned that her incurable obstinacy of thinking better of people than they deserved proved her judgment to be wrong. With unabandoned hope she tried a second letter and wrote also to Mary, who had sent Claire fifteen napoleons of the money she had earned through *The Liberal*.

"I am distressed," she wrote, "to think that poor Claire's melancholy state should diminish the small means of subsistence which you propose at present, though the feelings which induce you to share them with her would reward you for the privations it might occasion—my hope was that Lord B. on hearing of her state would from his (comparative) abundance, supply some positive relief— perhaps he has done so—if not, give him the enclosed & in what effect it may have—at all events it can do no one any harm, and I feel my motives to be so pure that I can not repent my importunity; though I may regret the discovery of his character being what I did not suppose it. . . .

"That Claire gave him reason to be enraged I have no doubt, & that the bitterness of her words [when she wrote to him after the death of Allegra][13] should have made him exceptionally angry, I do not wonder: but that he should hate her as he does, I cannot understand. I could not hate the Devil so, if he had torn at my heart with his claws & trampled on it with his cloven foot. I leave my letter open that you may read it if you please— from me you would never have known a word of the affair if he had chosen to keep his own counsel—but I am glad he did not, as you may follow up the game successfully, which I started—and you might not have liked to be the first to break the ice on a subject of this sort. . . . Lord B. if he does nothing for C[laire] will always consider me as a troublesome old Harridan, venturing to meddle in other peoples affairs: but if his generous feeling is moved to assist her effectually, I have no doubt he will hereafter feel thankful to his invisible adviser."[14]

Byron's reply to the second letter demonstrated that he was neither thankful to his adviser nor moved by generous feelings, and Mrs. Mason decided to trouble him no more, crediting his assurance of not meaning to offend her and being glad to part in peace. Yet the sneers in his letters (which have not been found) rankled, and she wrote to Mary finally on the subject: "As to Lord B[yron] I have done with him—a man who could wish to turn over upon you, with the uncertain supply of your own talents at this moment, or to me, who have not as many hundreds in the year as he has thousands, the performance of *his duty*—is incorrigible. I can only say that I do *not* 'envy him his feelings.' I do not regret what I have done, for I should have blamed myself if I had not done it, but I regret the disappearance of that illusion which (in spite of all I had heard) was still kept up by the perusal of his writings. I will read no more of his poetry for I shall always think him 'a counterfeit & no true man.' He may roll in riches or get drunk with fame, but he will never be happy. I have done with him for ever."[15]

Mrs. Mason herself felt with Claire and Mary the pinch of money matters, for Lord Mount Cashell had died suddenly in Ireland on October 27, 1822, at the age of fifty-one, and her annuity had stopped. The continuance of the annuity depended upon the good will of her eldest son, the third earl, but she was sanguine. "I suppose before long I must know something," she wrote to Mary in June of 1823, "as my eldest son & his family consisting of two daughters & a wife ready to augment the number, are gone to Ireland. R[obert, her favorite son] says she appears to be a good kind of woman & was well received by his family, which I was very glad to hear."[16] The next month she again wrote, "My affairs are not yet settled; but they will be to my satisfaction in time, for every thing I hear of my eldest son is honest & honourable & I am assured that his wife is a very amiable woman." (His wife had been the former Miss Anna Maria Wyss, of Bern, Switzerland.) In the meantime, the Masons lived as economically as possible on Tatty's income. A long letter to Mary dated March 4, 1823, shows Mrs. Mason again in the role of Minerva. "My dear Mary," she wrote,

"The contents of your last letter have disappointed me much, as I did not think it possible that Sir Timothy Shelley could be guilty of such an indecorous act as refusing the means of subsistence to his son's widow; but I still think that if you were in England he must be shamed into giving you something. I always was of opinion that you ought to have appeared there as soon as possible; but you were so averse to this plan, and Lord Byron's view of the affair was so plausible, that I did not press my advice—at all events, you have had the satisfaction of keeping your little Boy in a less severe climate during this dreadful winter; and I hope it is not too late for you to do all that might have been done at first. Surely some of the relations of your deceased husband (uncles, aunts, or cousins) must be reasonable beings, and they would see the propriety of Sir Timothy to behave *decently* on this occasion. All this you will find out when you are on the spot. Why not employ Mr. Medwin to go to the old gentleman?

"Lord Byron's advice of accepting the offer for the Child (that is to say, *appearing to do so*, for in such a case temporizing is necessary) is right; but you can say that, though willing to do everything which can conciliate for him the protection of his grandfather, you cannot think it right to deprive a child so young and delicate as he is of the care of his mother, and therefore you are content to *live with him* wherever Sir Timothy chooses to appoint; but I would not recommend you to say anything of this sort until you are in England. You ask my opinion, and therefore I give it; but I am by no means sure that it is the best. You will hear what others say. All you have to do at present is to write word that you are going to England with your child as soon as the season permits, and, however strong your determination of not separating from him, you had better not express it unless you find it absolutely necessary to do so. There are certain obstinate people who have a particular pleasure in forcing others to act contrary to their declared resolutions, and I should suspect Sir Timothy to be one of those. As to their taking the Child from you, I should suppose that impossible, unless they could prove something in your conduct to show you an improper person to be entrusted with the care of him, and that they cannot do, so clear as you have kept of politics and religion in your writings. When once you are in England, you will have better advisers than either Lord Byron or myself; and I sincerely hope you may receive such counsel as will lead to a comfortable arrangement before long. I have a *presentiment* in your favour.

"I have no letter from poor Clare, and my only hope respecting her is that the physician may have exaggerated very much, to enhance his own merit; though, to say the truth, I think it very likely that this is not the case; and, if so, there is little prospect of her recovery. At any rate, she cannot want the assistance of medical advice or drugs after the money you so generously sent to her, and till the month of May it would be of no advantage to her to remove to the sea. I will let you know what I hear of her health from herself or others.

"As to you, I expect no change in your circumstances till you are in England, where I hope you will go as soon as ever the weather is fine enough to undertake a journey northwards, without injury to the health of your child or yourself. I feel for the dreary prospect before you; but I think it will be only temporary, and perhaps the little Boy will be much the better for a cool summer. As to literary gain, you will certainly be more in the way of that in England than here, and the advantage of your

Father's advice and experience on subjects of this nature will be very great. I hope, however, that your abode in his house will not be very long; and for a short time all will go well, you may be sure. Mrs. Godwin has written with great kindness about you for the last year, and especially in the last six or seven months. I have no doubt you will find many people ready to offer their services, when you are near Sir Timothy, who would forget you while at a distance. I fear you will be gone before I shall be able to send you the medical book, for though I know it is published, I have heard nothing from the bookseller, and do not suppose they have sent the copies I desired to Livorno. Mrs. Williams probably has got hers by this time.

"My health continues more delicate than it was this time last year, and I know nothing of my affairs, which rather annoys me. Laurette and Nerina are well, and so is T[atty]. I suppose you saw in the papers the death of an old lady. Let me hear from you soon, and always believe me very / Truly yours, / M."[17]

The Masons spent the summer of 1823 at the Baths of Pisa, by coincidence in the same house (Casa Prinni, owned by Signora Turbati) that the Shelleys had occupied in 1820 and 1821. She and the girls had the first floor, and Tatty the second. Her health improved, although she was still something of an invalid and had not been able to eat meat for over a year. Tatty felt better, too; and the children thrived. One night she dreamed of Shelley "in one of his most brilliant humours" and felt a pang on awakening.[18]

Byron and Trelawny were planning to go to Greece to take part in the Greek War of Independence; *The Liberal* was to be discontinued after its fourth issue; and Mary made up her mind to return to England with her son. She waited first for good traveling weather and then for the delivery of Mrs. Hunt's child. When Vincent Hunt was born on June 9, Mary told Byron that she was ready to go, and he promised her the means. But she waited in vain for the money, and when Hunt reminded him that he owed Shelley £1,000—Byron and Shelley had agreed that whoever came into his inheritance first was to pay the other that sum—Byron became extravagant and angry, and Mary took offense. Then she appealed to Trelawny, who replied without any fuss, "Tell me what sum you want."[19] Mrs. Mason found it hard to believe that Byron had let Mary down after all his promises. Her own annuity had been stopped for almost a year and she was living sparingly, but she was still able to be of help and volunteered. "My dear Mary," she wrote from the Baths of Pisa in a letter dated "Sunday":

"I am quite shocked at the letter I have just received from you, for I did not think such a finale in the list of possibilities, after Lord B[yron] having prevented you from going to England with Mrs. W[illiams] as in prudence you ought to have done. What he says or thinks of me I care not—he cannot understand me—& I quite mistook him when I did him the honor of supposing that the words of truth and humanity from an indifferent person could have made any impression on him—but it was not to write of him that I took up my pen. I only wished to tell you how sincerely I regret not having it in my power to offer you the effectual aid I could wish & to say that having (by means not worth relating) a sum of thirty zecchini of which I can dispose without consulting anyone, you are heartily welcome to it—so that if nothing better turns out (I still think it possible Lord B. may behave decently) before this letter reaches you, write to me instantly the address of some merchant in Genoa to whom it can be paid as that would probably be the speediest method—you will then have less to borrow from Mr. Trelawny & I hope you will thus be enabled to set off for England without further loss of time—as to this money, if you are ever a rich woman, you shall repay it—if you are not, you need never think more about it. Be assured I have not ceased to think kindly of you since your misfortunes, which indeed have shown you in a more amiable point of view than ever I saw you in before—but alas! there are cases in which sympathy avails not, & this is one of them. I am in such haste to send this that I can only add the sincere good wishes / of yours very truly / M."[20]

On July 17 Byron and Trelawny sailed for Greece, "Lord Byron with £10,000, Trelawny with £50," in Mary's words. Byron gave her no money, nor did he say farewell; but Trelawny gave her what she requested, and Mrs. Mason sent her the thirty *zecchini*. On July 25 Mary and her son left for England. Mrs. Mason was eager that Mary take with her a new medical book published by Longman in January of 1823 entitled *Advice to Young Mothers on the Physical Education of Children* By a Grandmother. The grandmother-author was Mrs. Mason.

The interest she had in medicine was first awakened by Mary Wollstonecraft, who had taught that women as well as men should be physicians. For thirty years Mrs. Mason had pursued the subject, observing medical practices in Ireland, England, France, Italy, Germany, and Austria, reading medical books in the various languages, associating with physicians and corresponding with them both in Europe and America. She had borne ten children, and she had for eight years provided poor Italians with the benefit of her medical knowledge and experience. This knowledge she put into some three hundred and fifty pages of a book that she wished had been available when she herself was twenty. Most of the books on child care before her time had been concerned with moral rather than physical education, and eighteenth-century medical books both amuse and appall the modern reader with the witches' brews they seriously recommend. A viper, if not the eye of newt, was a not uncommon ingredient—easily procured at the apothecary's—for an eighteenth-century tonic.

It is marvelous how modern (if that word is entirely complimentary) Mrs. Mason's views are on nursing, diet, exercise, fresh air, preventive medicine, and child psychology. She begins with advice to the mother during pregnancy and then advises on principles of physical and mental hygiene to be pursued until the child reaches the age of fifteen. One hundred and twenty-three years after the book was published, a modern mother, upon reading Mrs. Mason's remarks on praise and censure of the child, said, "Excellent! I wish I had been as aware."

Vaccà was among those who received the book with enthusiasm, and Madame Vaccà was converted to nursing her own child. He thought that a woman of good sense who studied the book would need no physician for her children, and that there was a great deal in the book of which many physicians were ignorant. "None but a medical man," he said, "could be perfectly aware of the merit of that part of the book which treats of diseases."[21] Subsequent editions appeared in Boston (1833), London (1835), Florence (1835), and Leghorn (1840).

One copy of the first edition has an interesting history. It was purchased in London in 1828 by Gabriele Rossetti to help with the raising of his children, Dante, William Michael, and Christina. When William Michael had children of his own, his mother wrote on the flyleaf, "For William From His Mother"; and his daughters, Helen and Olivia, were brought up on Mrs. Mason's *Advice*. Italians in England were helped to raise their children by an Irish-woman in Italy.

CHAPTER 11.

Mrs. Mason's letter to Mary on March 4 contained the sentence, "I suppose you saw in the papers the death of an old lady." The old lady was her mother, the Dowager Countess of Kingston, who died in London on January 13, 1823, and was buried in Putney Churchyard. As granddaughter and sole heiress of the fourth Baron Kingston, she had brought her husband the White Knight's property at Mitchelstown, which reverted to her upon her husband's death in 1799. Her eldest son, Big George, became the third Earl of Kingston at once, but he also coveted the property, and to deprive his mother of it he instituted fierce and expensive legal proceedings which continued for over fifty years. During the twenty-four years that Lady Kingston survived her husband, Big George was unsuccessful and impatient. The good countess, in turn, was unsuccessful in her design to disinherit him entirely, for the property was entailed and had to go to him when she died.

His position in his father's family seems to have been less than that of eldest son. As a young man he had run off with Miss Johnstone and had been brought back to marry Lady Helena Moore. He had been on hand to sport with the North Cork Militia in '98, but he was not

on hand to defend his sister's honor when Colonel Fitz-
Gerald seduced her. His younger brother Robert had sent
the challenge, faced FitzGerald's pistol in Hyde Park,
and pursued FitzGerald to the inn at Kilworth. When
the second earl died, Robert—not George—inherited the
estate at Rockingham, and George had to wait for twenty-
four years to inherit the estate at Mitchelstown.

He had waited a long time to come into his own, but
when he did, he came in with a roar. Upon his mother's
death, he summoned his architect, Mr. Paine of Cork City,
and ordered him to construct a castle that would be a fitting habitation for himself and a setting worthy to entertain King George IV. "Build me a castle," he said, as
Aubrey DeVere tells the story in his *Recollections*. "I
am no judge of architecture; but it must be larger than
any other house in Ireland, and have an entrance tower to
be named 'the White Knight's Tower.' No delay! It
is time for me to enjoy."

At once the castle built by his father in 1776 was razed,
and work on the new edifice began. All the inhabitants of
Mitchelstown shared in the £100,000 Big George was
spending. The new Tower of the White Knight was rising proudly into the air when a wealthy manufacturer
built an enormous chimney in the square of the town and
declined to remove the rival spire as the Earl of Kingston
commanded. George drove into the town and addressed
the crowd that, caps in hand, had gathered round his
carriage. "I have come to wish you good-bye, boys," he
said with regret. "This place is but a small place, and
there is not room in it for me and that man (pointing toward the chimney). He says the law is on his side, and
I dare say it is. Consequently, I go to England tomorrow." That very night a group of uninvited guests paid
their respects to the wealthy manufacturer, who changed

his mind about the chimney and left town within three days.

In the record time of three years the castle of hewn stone was finished. Castellated, neo-Gothic, with twin square towers one hundred and six feet high, Mitchelstown Castle was the largest private residence in Ireland. The stately gallery eighty feet in length was the scene of the first great housewarming, over which Big George presided. But George IV, who was too well entertained in Dublin, never paid his call.

The next great gathering in the gallery was the last for many a year. The Irish Catholics had been emancipated in 1829, and George rode over to Limerick to see that his tenants were the first to vote in the election, never dreaming that they would vote for anybody but his candidate. A mile-long file of Kingston tenants rode by on horseback, cheered their lord as he drank champagne— and voted for his rival to a man. Big George was stunned. He sat brooding in his castle while couriers scoured the estate ordering the tenants to assemble. Enthroned on a dais at one end of the gallery, he fixed his eye on the tenants as they pressed nearer and nearer while the gallery filled. The last time a mob had pressed round him was in '98 in Wexford. That mob had a pitchcap on the top of a pike and was crying for his life, but then he was protected by a barricade and armed men. Now the tenants were respectfully attending to what their chieftain would say, when suddenly he threw his hands on high and cried, "They are come to tear me in pieces; they are come to tear me in pieces!" Kind people took him from the White Knight's Tower to a madhouse, where he was treated well for the remainder of his life.[1]

2

With the Shelley circle thoroughly dispersed, Casa
Silva settled back to its former repose: Tatty on the second
floor, Mrs. Mason and the children on the first.   Mrs.
Mason's health was almost always poor, and in her letters
to Mary she speaks of headaches, inflammation of the
liver, and coughs, sometimes accompanied by spitting
blood.   One winter she was confined to the house for
three months, and to bed for four weeks; but her spirits
were almost always good.   Rather than allow herself to
be idle, she cared for her house and children as well as
for her poor Italian patients, and she worked on two new
medical books she was encouraged to attempt after the
success of her *Advice to Young Mothers*.   She also undertook the translation of certain medical works from the
German, a task for which few were as well qualified as she.
Most people who had her knowledge of German and of
medicine did not have the leisure to undertake translation.[2]

During the winter of 1823 she was bed-ridden much
of the time and amused herself by writing a two-volume
novel, *The Sisters of Nansfield: A Tale for Young Wom-
en*, which was published by Longman in November of
1824.   She considered it "trifling," but it was received
with approbation.[3]   The story is about two young ladies:
Harriet Maynard, who was seventeen, and her sister
Fanny, fifteen.   Their father prided himself on his kinship
with nobility, but when he was accidentally killed, his wife
discovered that he had more noble blood than money and
that she had to live with her daughters on the one small
farm that was left them.   Fanny had a propensity to ridicule and a quickness in discovering the faults of her
acquaintances; whereas Harriet had a love of dress, of

flattery, and of fashion. Harriet, who was unhappy in humble circumstances, could not quite agree that it was much pleasanter to go into the garden and gather a salad for supper than to sit looking at a stupid card table in a shut-up room. Her real trouble began when she deceived her mother and eloped with Edwin Rowland. After Edwin's death, she returned to her relatives, who forgave her the grief she had caused herself and them. But her story was not forgotten. Fanny overcame her faults and married a fine young man, quite properly with banns and all.

The Godwins wanted to bring out another edition of *Old Daniel* and commissioned two more stories in order to secure the copyright. The book had been selling well and delighting children since 1807, and a second volume, *Continuation of the Stories,* had appeared. Mrs. Mason wrote to Mary Shelley on November 29 (1824). "I am very much obliged to you for the Posthumous Works [of Shelley] & should have written to thank you two months ago, but delayed from day to day in hopes of being able to tell you that my head was well enough to attempt the two stories you requested for the first Vol. of O.D. This was not the case till within these few days—however I can now tell you that the stories are finished & I have only to copy them out & send them by an opportunity which I expect to have for Paris next week. I hope they may answer the purpose & think it probable that they will, though I am not particularly delighted with them myself —it was so long since I had attempted anything in that stile or indeed since I had written any thing but letters (almost a year) that I found myself quite at a loss how to begin—they may be inserted between the *Little Peddler* & the *Manhater*—and I only hope they are not too late— but my head was in such a state, that two or three times when I attempted to fix my attention, my eyes & whole forehead became so painful that I could not look at anything—my health is very much improved within this last month, & though the liver complaint is not quite removed, yet I have been able to leave off hemlock at last & hope by degrees to be as well as half the old women one meets."[4]   But the stories arrived in London too late or were not satisfactory and never appeared; and when the same fate befell two more stories she attempted, Mrs. Mason thought she would put the four together and make another book for Nerina's own use.

In England Mary Shelley still had worries about supporting herself and her boy in the face of Sir Timothy's obstinate parsimony.   He objected to seeing Mary's name in print; yet he would not give her enough money to make it unnecessary for her to write.   Mrs. Mason's letters to Mary were always sanguine, holding out the hope that seemed to point to better things just around the corner. "I have received both your letters my Dear Mary," she wrote, "& am very glad indeed that you have at last got even a small settlement; especially as your future prospects are so good, in consequence of the certainty that there is no idea of attempting to set aside your husband's will—in regard to your imprisonment among the John Bulls, in all probability it is not likely to last very long, as a man of Sir T[imothy]'s age & character with a chronic disease such as the gout cannot be likely to hold out a great many years; and when you are a rich woman you will travel to Italy with more comfort than you could at present."[5]   But Sir Timothy lived on spitefully to be ninety-two, and Mary did not receive the inheritance Shelley left her until 1844.

Claire Clairmont had gone from Vienna to Russia, much against Mrs. Mason's advice.   She told Claire that she herself would rather sit behind Mrs. Godwin's counter in the book shop from morning till night than to be any-one's *dame de compagnie,* and she also warned her about the Russians.[6] But Claire would never agree on the subject, and off she went to predicted discontent. "If she could be persuaded of the expediency of returning to her own country," Mrs. Mason thought, "for the purpose of resigning part of her legacy [which Shelley had left her] for a present maintenance, perhaps that consideration might have an effect, as she might afterwards return to Italy or Germany or go to any other place she liked."[7] Claire remained in Russia for four years.

Lord Byron and Trelawny had, of course, gone off to Greece, Byron to die of fever and Trelawny to be severely wounded. As Byron lay dying, his servant heard him say something about leaving Claire a settlement. "Your ac-count of Lord B's sufferings make me pity him—," Mrs. Mason wrote to Mary. "It is unlucky he was not able to write what he attempted to say to his servant. . . . Do you remember my last letter to Lord B. & what I said of 'the sleepless bed of pain'? It appears to have been prophetic. I regret having written it, as it was to no purpose—but my motive was good, & it might have had an effect."[8] Trelawny returned to England, bringing with him his fifteen-year-old Greek wife.

In the autumn of 1823, Mrs. Mason and Tatty ac-quired the Villa Archinto outside the Porta alla Piaggia in the suburb of San Michele, a house which the Shelleys had once thought of taking. It was a little house suitable only for summer residence, but large enough to allow Tatty to have the second floor inviolably to himself. They spent the summer of 1824 there, moving back to Casa Silva, furniture and all, as autumn approached. In June Mrs. Mason wrote her will, using her legal name, and referring to Laurette and Nerina as her "young friends" rather than as her daughters. The will shows, too, that she had contact with, and confidence in, her eldest daughter, Lady Helena.

"I MARGARET JANE MOUNT CASHELL widow of Stephen Earl of Mount Cashell of Ireland being of sound and sane mind though weak in bodily health do make this my last Will and Testament on this fifteenth day of June A.D. eighteen hundred and twenty four in the manner following. I give and bequeathe to my excellent and beloved daughter Helena Eleanor Wife of Richard Robinson Esqr. (oldest son of Sir John Robinson, Bart) all my effects of what kind or nature soever or wheresoever situate or being what I have or shall have in trust for my young friends Anna Laura Georgina Tighe (usually called Laurette) and Catherine Elizabeth Raniera Tighe (usually called Nerina) now residing with me at Pisa in Tuscany relying on my beloved daughter the said Helena Eleanor Robinson to act in this matter as she knows I should wish her to do and I appoint her and her worthy husband the said Richard Robinson Esqr. EXECUTORS of this my last Will and Testament which I have written with my own hand by which I revoke all former Wills made by me IN WITNESS whereof I have hereunto set my hand this 15th day of June A.D. 1824/MARGARET JANE MOUNT CASHELL"[9]

In March of the next year after taking the Villa Archinto, Mrs. Mason received news which at first seemed to be bad: the owner of Casa Silva decided to sell the property to a Russian general and to turn out Mrs. Mason from the house she had lived in for ten years. At first it startled her to be uprooted, but the more she thought of it the gladder she became for a thousand reasons. The Villa Archinto was winterized with chimneys, a fireplace, and seven stoves; and in May of 1825 the family moved permanently into the villa. The more they saw of it the more delightful it seemed.[10]   When Thomas Jefferson Hogg, Shelley's friend, visited Pisa in October, he occupied the spare bedroom on Tatty's floor. Mrs. Mason said that she liked Hogg because he was odd and ready to be pleased. "He looks like an Englishman, but does not talk of foreign nations like one," said the woman who had become Italian and could not imagine why anybody would want to live anywhere other than in Italy.[11]

An oddly worded sentence in a letter to Mary referred to an illness that had been provokingly incurred; "but as it is a long story," Mrs. Mason wrote, "& concerning an individual unknown to you (a near relation of mine),"[12] she would not go into details. Another oddly worded, undated, and unposted note found among Tatty's papers may refer to this same illness. It seems to be addressed to a brother of Mrs. Mason, who, like many another, had fallen in love with Madame Lebrun. The precise cause of indignation is not so clear as the indignation itself.

The note says, "I return the coral necklaces sent by you from Naples, which were of infinite value in my estimation while they appeared to be a pledge of your good will towards my children; but since they prove to have been only intended for the friends of Madame Lebrun, you cannot be surprized that I will not suffer Laurette & Nerina to keep them any longer. I grieve most truly for your unfortunate infatuation & have scarcely a doubt that you will one day regret having sacrificed to such an idol the esteem and affection of your Friend & Sister / M."[13]

The Kingston men were as successful with women as they were susceptible to their charms. Big George had run off with Miss Johnstone because it was a fine night to run away with another man's daughter, and a second

brother was noted for his amours in Austria. Prince
Pückler-Muskau in his *Tour in England, Ireland, and
France* tells of having known one of Mrs. Mason's
brothers in Vienna. "He was a remarkably handsome
man," Pückler-Muskau wrote, "and celebrated for his
'bonnes fortunes'; at one time the avowed lover of the
Duchess of ———, whom he treated with so little ceremony, that once when he invited me to breakfast at the
hotel where they were living, I found the Duchess alone,
and he came into the room some time after, in dressing
gown and slippers, out of his or their chamber."[14] If
this refers to the Honorable John King, Secretary of the
Embassy to the Elector of Würtemberg, his lady would
appear to be the Duchess of Würtemberg, daughter of
George III. Lady Kingston used to walk on the terrace
at Windsor with her.

Really, it is difficult not to feel that the quiet life
Mrs. Mason led was not happier and more useful than
the lives of her brothers: George with his castle in Ireland, John with his duchess in Vienna, and the third with
Madame Lebrun in Naples.

MRS. TIGHE

CHAPTER 12.

LORD MOUNT CASHELL's death at Moore Park in 1822 had put a stop to Mrs. Mason's annuity, but it also made it possible for her and Tatty to marry, although the marriage of two people who had been living together for seventeen years and who had two daughters would have to be celebrated with discreet privacy. The marriage did not take place until 1826, but the following letter shows that arrangements were attempted long before that date. The fact that this letter was found among Tatty's papers may indicate that it was not presented to the English chaplain at Leghorn to whom it was addressed. It was written at the Bagni di Casciano on May 27, 1823.

"My dear Sir / This note will be presented to you by Mr. Tighe and the Dowager Countess of Mount Cashell who had applied to me to perform the marriage ceremony, but whom I have referred to *you* as *alone* able to solemnize it *legally* .

"Peculiar circumstances require that the ceremony should be private, & you will therefore oblige both the parties & myself by being altogether silent on its having taken place unless, of course, if called upon to certify that it was regularly solemnized in the English Church at Leghorn. The parties will bring their necessary witnesses with them, so that beyond yourself, no person will be enabled to make the matter a subject of conversation, to prevent which annoyance these precautions are taken.

"We leave this for the Baths of Lucca on the 10th of June, & perhaps I shall before that time be enabled to get down to Leghorn to see you—if not this letter will I am sure answer the same purpose—meanwhile believe me / D[ea]r Sir / Very truly yrs / James Ellis."[1]

The three-year delay before the ceremony was performed is hard to understand, unless Mrs. Mason felt it impossible to be married by the resident British chaplain without some leak to the resident British gossips. At any rate, the marriage was delayed until March 6, 1826, when it was recorded in the Register Book of Marriages at Leghorn that "George William Tighe Esquire of Dublin, and Margaret Jane Moore Dowager Countess of Mt. Cashell were married in Villa Archinto the residence of G. W. Tighe Esqr. at Pisa in Tuscany" by Charles Neat, British Chaplain at Leghorn, in the presence of Francesco Tantini and William Jackson.[2]

The marriage, of course, made no difference in the daily lives of the family, not even enough to make Mrs. Mason change her name: she remained Mrs. Mason to her English correspondents and to her Italian friends. The new house, the Villa Archinto, continued to be a delight, exactly what Tatty wanted for his farming pursuits and what Mrs. Mason wanted for her obscurity. But another consideration was that Laurette, now a young lady of seventeen, needed more companions, particularly male companions, than the suburbs of Pisa could provide. Tatty did not agree with his wife on the subject of introducing Laurette into society, and there were discussions between the occupants of the first and second floors as to whether the family should not move back into Pisa during the winter months. The pupil of Mary Wollstonecraft was not one to give in to a man (especially when her position was one of rational common sense), nor was Tatty a man to give up his quiet life in the suburbs to expose himself to the society of Pisa. In 1826 he added a postscript to the last page of the autobiography he had previously written and which he had concluded with the sentence, "Certain it is that after many storms we now enjoy as much happiness as falls to the lot of most people."

"I am bound for the sake of truth," he wrote with some spleen, "to add that the last years of my life have been embitter'd by constant altercations which I think will end in separation & have a vast influence on the Educations & Fortunes of the Children.

"My wish for many years past has been to bring up the children in perfect Retirement till Laurette reached the age of 20.

"To save money during that time for the purpose of adding to their very small means.

"To have a decent & tolerably well regulated House in proportion to our means.

"I have been thwarted in all these objects & after several years struggling I foresee that I shall never be able to carry any one of my points I had most set my Heart upon."[3]

In the fall of 1826 Mrs. Mason and the girls moved back into Pisa, while Tatty, who would not break through his habits of retirement, remained at the Villa. The two families visited each other, and sometimes Tatty came with flowers or prize potatoes that he had raised. During the summer months Mrs. Mason returned to the country. A few undated letters exchanged between town and country survive, and they shed light on the relations between the two households. One from Mrs. Mason to

Tatty tells him that he was expected in Pisa on Sunday and points out that some of his reasoning was "sophistical," a word which used to be a favorite with Mary Wollstonecraft. It is dated "Saturday" and begins, "My dear—

"Nerina was so much better last night that I now hope her convalescence will go on smoothly. She is not the better for getting up on Thursday (to which her uneasiness & impatience had forced my unwilling consent) and yesterday had prudence enough to desire to remain in bed & this morning I expect a great improvement in her health. My cold is almost gone. I told you that a part of your letter had appeared to me *sophistical*—the passage is this —after talking of the possibility of your turning your property into an annuity & obtaining a thousand a year, you say, 'if I were to do so & to spend the whole of such income, providing only for the present maintenance of the children, I should then do no more than what you are doing at this moment.' I must say that this is a very unfair statement of the case, as it is a very unlikely thing that I should spend my whole income if I had not to maintain the children, or if I supposed they had no future means of support but what I should be able to save for them—besides counting on their inheriting your estate in Ireland, I always imagined that out of your 600£ a year you saved 300£ and therefore that I might safely spend my whole income for two or three years, and give Laurette an opportunity of being married by having her be seen & known.

"We expect you to dine here tomorrow & hope to have a respectable plumb pudding to meet you. I do not think Nerina will be fit to remove before Tuesday & will consult Doctor Appolloni on the subject when she appears to me well enough—she has slept well & is still asleep, & if the slight perspiration which she had all day yesterday should have continued through the night, I expect to find the swelling much diminished this morning.

"Your note is just come but Nerina still sleeps so I can tell you nothing more of her. We all expect you to-morrow & the cake is not to be cut till you come."[4]

The new mode of life agreed with Mrs. Mason to such an extent that she did not keep her bed one day through the winter. Instead she indulged in *stravaganze* that she had not dreamed of in twenty years. During Carnival she had young people dancing in her house until three in the morning and was none the worse for staying with them, and she also went to the theater; but the family held firm to its policy of not mixing in English society. Laurette was allowed to attend some balls that were given by the Haitian Principality ("they are very amicable persons these same black ladies," Mrs. Mason said, "and I often see them"), but Laurette did not go to the English parties even though they were especially gay that season.[5] When Mary Shelley's friends, the Gisbornes, planned a trip to Pisa, Mrs. Mason begged Mary not to give them a letter of introduction, for, though she was no longer living like a hermit, her society was quite Italian.[6] Thus she protected her daughter against the possibility of meeting prudes armed with weapons of humiliation.

She was well pleased with the results of having her girls live in the city. When she wrote to Mary Shelley on September 16 (1827), she was back at the Villa Archinto for the summer, but preparing to return to Pisa the next month. "You would indeed find my girls greatly altered," she wrote. "Laurette, whom you left an awkward timid child, is now a fine young woman, free from that excessive bashfulness which even one twelvemonth ago made her appear almost silly; her manners have been improved by conversing with human creatures of various sorts [which ought to convince even Tatty that living in Pisa was a good thing], and she enjoyed the dancing and other amusements of the last Carnival very much. At Madame Mastinni's she met many foreigners, but our society at home were almost all Italians; for many reasons I have made it a rule to receive no English. Nerina is growing up very well; she has been a very idle little thing, but within the last few months is quite altered, and now pays great attention to her masters and everything I wish her to learn. She is very observing, and has more the appearance of being clever than Laurette had at her age, but is much inferior in acquirements; her father has never taken her education in hand, and I am much less strict, believing it to be of little importance whether certain necessary matters, such for instance as arithmetic, are learnt a year sooner or a year later. Nerina is quite an Italian, and excessively fond of music; indeed so is Laurette also." She then goes on to say that she and the girls were going to move into Pisa, to the Casa Lupi on the Via San Lorenzo, near the Piazza Santa Caterina, a part of the town she liked very much.[7]

The next month the Masons moved into Casa Lupi, which was to be a literary center just as Casa Silva had been the focal point of Shelley's circle a few years earlier, except that this time the members of the group were for the most part Italians. On October 26, 1827, the *Accademia dei Lunatici*, or Academy of Lunatics, held the first of its fortnightly meetings, which continued until April 23, 1832.[8] It cannot be entirely a coincidence that many of the forty-six members later played important roles in the history of the Italian *Risorgimento*, and one is tempted to trace the liberalism of Mary Wollstonecraft into Italy by way of Mrs. Mason. Some of the members who later distinguished themselves were Giuseppe Giusti,

Antonio Guadagnoli, Bartolomeo Cini, Angelica Palli, Tommaso Gherardi, Antonio Mordini, Giuseppe Montanelli, Ferdinando Zannetti, Silvio Orlandini, and Francesco Guerrazzi. Many of these were at the time students at the University of Pisa, the more important of the two Tuscan universities.

The purpose of the Academy was to provide a pleasant literary pastime without giving undue importance to the literary compositions in prose or verse that were read by the Academicians. Each member adopted the name of a constellation and received an elegantly lithographed emblem, or certificate of membership, which contained the words, "If you are not crazy we do not want you." The laws of the Academy, similar to the laws of other Italian academies of the time, stated that each new member was to be elected after having been proposed by a member, that the discussions were not to be "tumultuous," and that manuscripts read at the meetings were to become the property of the Academy.

At the first meeting, an Academic Senate consisting of four officers was elected:

President   Margherita Mason, *Bilancia*
Vice-President Pietro Koster, *Ercole*
Archivist   Lauretta Tighe, *Sagittaria*
Secretary   Alessandro Rosselmini, *Centauro*

The ritual for admission of a new member might not appeal to those who took themselves seriously. The candidate made written application: "I, ———, desiring to be received among these most respectable Lunatics, and flattering myself on possessing the necessary qualities to obtain a place in their illustrious Academy, present myself now to request admission."

The secretary then asked the candidate, "Have you examined the motto of the Society?"

"Yes."

"Then do you confess to be crazy?"

"I so confess."

"Who vouches for you?"

"Lunatic A. B."

Thereupon the Academicians voted their decision.

Giuseppe Giusti was a law student at the University when he became a member. The Acts of the Academy contain several of his early poems, most of which scarcely indicate that he was to become a most distinguished writer, an author of classic satire, and an underminer of Austrian rule in Italy. The following poem,[9] which was read by the young student to the assembled Lunatics, though not a very good poem even in the original Italian, does hint at the penetrating, personal quality of attack which was to make him feared and famous. The second lady of the poem is Mrs. Mason; the first remains mercifully unidentified.

THE ART OF BEING OBNOXIOUS

There lived (although I know not in what place)
 A lady of the rarest quality
Who cultivated lit'rature apace
 While yet a babe upon her mother's knee.
What fame she found among the human race,
 Exploiting letters in society,
If you will listen as you would to birds,
I'll tell you all in two well-chosen words.

She early wed a harmless little man,
 Who might have been a Canon of the Duomo
He did so little bad—or good—in his life's span.
 But he was nice to have about the home, O.
(For who would dare abuse a gentleman
 For having nothing solid in his dome, O?)

In faith and morals he was orthodox;
His name was Bert, and hers was Chatterbox.

Oh, if I had the artist's gift and brush
    I would portray that amiable face
Just when with learned air without a blush
    She puts her wretched victim in his place.
Sometimes with friendly mocking she will crush;
    Sometimes she'll charm you; other times debase.
She beckons here and there like a coquette,
A gibbering monkey or a marionette.

What bit of gossip could be advertised
    Of which she didn't know the entire story?
What written book has she not criticized—
    The Abacus, the Bible in its glory,
The history of Rome epitomized?
    In short, no Tuscan, Hebrew, Whig, or Tory
Has writ a book unknown to her, I'll bet,
Unless it be the Book of Etiquette.

She knows the Turkish and the Chinese rites;
    She knows that Adam and Eve wore sandals;
She knows the art, the thought, the hidden sites
    Of the Etruscans, Erules, and the Vandals.
But the chief gift which lifts her to the heights
    Consists in telling lies and spreading scandals.
To call this gift a fault would be unfit:
She proves her talent for inventive wit.

Trecento taught her in its golden school
    To shun new syntax, linguistically wary.
God help you if you ever break a rule
    Or use a word not in *her* dictionary.
With irony she'll make you out a fool
    Attack, assault you till you're more than chary,

And stupefied stay silent as a clam,
Her victim vanquished with an epigram.

This lady had accomplishments so rare
 That many thought her like an oracle.
Her sermons seemed to them beyond compare—
 They gaped in wonder at the spectacle.
But then she'd make such blunders that, I swear,
 All were struck dumb but for a miracle.
Forgive these human, pardonable defects,
Inseparable from man—and the fair sex.

Another lady dwelt in this same place
 Wise, cultured, pleasing, full of smiles;
Whose love of learning caused her to embrace
 None of the usual tricks of women's wiles.
She gathered friends together with good grace,
 United them from the surrounding miles,
Called for a vote; and then with one assent
The Academicians made her president.

Now since this lady had no use for men
 Who pass through life without a grain of sense,
Presume to wisdom, learning, culture—then
 Encourage praise of their intelligence,
She wished the Academicians in her ken
 To pose as fools—but just in self-defense.
The members straight decided to assume
The Tutelary Genius of the Moon.

By common vote of every gay buffoon
 To keep the circle going once 'twas made,
On every second Monday, by the Moon,
 Assembled all the amiable brigade.
When Chatterbox found out—and that was soon—
 That she herself had not quite made the grade,

To venge herself, and all the fools to curse,
She wrote a bitter sonnet in free verse.

Then up and down and round about she went
    To damn the group and put a pox upon it.
She spluttered in her rage and tried to vent
    Her spleen in declamation of her sonnet.
But people of good sense would not consent
    To harken to the bee within her bonnet.
Instead they thought the Furies had the bore,
And pushed the learned lady out the door.

Poor Chatterbox!   For this outrageous act
    The wonder is she did not drop down dead,
Had not one feeble ray of hope abstract
    Impregnated her pointed little head.
Ah Chatterbox, take heart, cheer up, react!
    They've thrown you out, but do not die; instead,
Invoke your angry Muse; think well upon it,
And crush them with a sesta rima sonnet.

Therefore, for posing as a doctoress
    And putting everybody in a fix
My learned magpie was denied access
    To the Academy of Lunatics.
Ladies, you too will be in like distress
    If one of you————why be prolix?
I'll write you now no moralistic verse;
Instruct yourself for better or for worse.

                                CERBERO

On May 12, 1828, Alessandro Rosselmini proposed
a new member, Count Giacomo Leopardi. Leopardi, the
author of impassioned verse, had been living in Pisa since
November and now was admitted to the Academy of
Lunatics. Mrs. Mason must have seen in him many of

the characteristics of Shelley: he was a sickly and sensitive genius, a Hellene, and a pessimist capable of writing poetry combining great dignity with passion. She could not have foreseen, though, that the twentieth century would consider his work superior to the work of the English poet whom he resembled. Leopardi must have looked twice at the pretty Irish girls with Italian names, one called Laura—beloved of Petrarch, the other called Nerina—beloved of Leopardi.

His diary gives an account of a meeting he attended at Casa Lupi when the burlesque poet Guadagnoli recited some of his own verses, accentuating the ridiculousness with mimicry and gesture. Leopardi's temperament was not such as to allow him to be amused by a young man "laughing at himself, at his own youth, at his own misfortunes, exposing himself to ridicule for the entertainment of others." Instead he thought it "the saddest of all forms of despair." After he left Pisa at the end of June, he remained a corresponding member, exchanged letters with "Madama Mason," and frequently asked that he be remembered to her in his letters to the other Academicians.[10]

In 1830 Mrs. Mason moved from Casa Lupi to a large house she rented from Carlo Zanetti, "*Maestro di Musica*," at 1069 Via della Faggiola.[11] To this house Claire Clairmont came early in 1832. Claire had spent a wandering decade since Shelley had died—Vienna, Moscow, London, Dresden, Carlsbad, Nice, unreal cities without distractions to distract her from the memory of Shelley and Allegra. Now, after ten years, she returned to her Minerva. Mrs. Mason gave her the royalties due from the sale of the *Advice to Young Mothers*, a sum of fourteen pounds, but Claire immediately offered the money to Mary Shelley, for cholera had broken out in

London and the distracted Claire wanted Mary to leave the city. Claire herself wanted to go to Vienna, but Mrs. Mason would not let her, considering her weak health, the fatigue of the journey, and the agony of depression she had endured for the past twelve years. Instead, Claire lived with the Masons and found a post as day governess with an English family.

Daily she went to her post at nine in the morning, not to return until ten at night. At that time she went directly to her room to avoid the acquaintance of the company of young men whom the Masons constantly entertained. In her room Claire read through the old, unhappy correspondence of the past and made "copies" of the letters her mother had written to Mrs. Mason. Sometimes she made two copies of a letter, and sometimes the two copies differed from each other.

"Nothing can equal Mrs. Mason's kindness to me," Claire wrote to Mary. "Hers is the only house, except my Mother's, in which all my life I have always felt at home. With her, I am as her child; from the merest trifle to the greatest object, she treats me as if her happiness depended on mine. Then she understands me so completely. I have no need to disguise my sentiments; to barricade myself up in silence, as I do almost with everybody, for fear they should see what passes in my mind, and hate me for it, because it does not resemble what passes in theirs. This ought to be a great happiness to me, and would, did not her unhappiness and her precarious state of health darken it with the torture of fear. It is too bitter, after a long life passed in unbroken misery, to find a good only that you may lose it. Laurette's marriage is to take place at the end of November."[12]

Laurette was engaged to Prince Adolfo Domenico Galloni d'Istria, of the French consular service. Much

as the two were in love, Mrs. Mason could not approve
of the marriage, for she felt, and rightly, that the scene-
making Galloni was unworthy of Laurette. It was the
first time that mother and daughter had disagreed, and
their quiet life had not vaccinated them against the rebuffs
and discord that less secluded people were prepared to
accept. The seventeen-year-old Nerina was at least as
much affected as the others whenever she saw her mother
and Laurette fix their eyes mournfully upon each other.
She would take Claire into her study and talk incessantly
of her hatred of Galloni, and then, after pouring out her
soul, the two would burst into laughter at the ridiculous
figures human beings cut. Nerina would preach much
eloquent nonsense to her young friends of both sexes, cen-
suring love, the male, and matrimony, for which institu-
tion she would substitute patriotism.[13] In spite of all
this, Laurette married Galloni in November of 1832 and
went to live in Genoa. The letters she wrote back home
said that she was happy.[14]

There was only one subject on which Claire and the
Masons disagreed. "They never see any English," she
wrote to Jane Williams, "and have the most unfounded
and ludicrous horror of them. . . . They had rather damn
all their fellow creatures in a lump than allow the evil
manners of the Italians. I never met with people so
prejudiced in certain ways as the Masons. They abhor
despotic governments on account of the blighting influence they have on the subjects of them, but when you
make their conclusions turn upon the Italians, they deny it
—no! no!—they have all the honour and uprightness
which distinguish republicans."[15] Claire had not been
born in Ireland, where an inexorable, vertical line separated nine-tenths of the people from society, property,
suffrage, and education.

All Nerina's talk against love, the male, and matrimony was only talk. Claire listened to her complaint on the faulty ways in which she had been educated, by which Nerina meant that her fluency in three languages, her accomplishment as a musician, and her love of literature would prevent her marrying "some blackbeard of an Italian" (Claire's phrase) who expected his wife to have no education other than that of sewing and reading a little.[16]   But Claire was quick to say that the two girls were "the noblest and most honourable characters," and she was among the first to realize that the Italian whom Nerina loved and married was worthy of her.

Nerina was eighteen when she married Bartolomeo Cini, "the best and most delightful Pistoiese,"[17] in January of 1834. They met when he was a law student at the University of Pisa and used to attend the literary salon conducted by Mrs. Mason. He was a member of an ancient Tuscan family, seated for some centuries at San Marcello in Pistoia, a family distinguished enough to entertain several European sovereigns, among them Leopold I of Tuscany, Peter Leopold of Austria, and Pope Pius VII. His father, Giovanni Cini, had in 1807 founded a paper mill, the *Cartiera della Lima,* to provide work for the people of San Marcello.[18]   Bartolomeo was destined to direct the work of this paper mill as his principal occupation, but he was, in addition, a young man of literary, scientific, and political interests. Nerina, the Italian patriot, could not have found a better man to put a stop to her talk against love and marriage.

The marriage contract was drawn up on January 18, by which Nerina received a dowry of two thousand pounds sterling, amounting to 33,600 Tuscan florins, and an additional 5,400 florins from Mrs. Mason.[19]   The wedding was a Catholic ceremony, for Nerina had adopted the

religion of her native country. The couple left for San
Marcello, leaving behind them a mother happy and at
ease. With his two daughters married to Italians, Tatty
set about disposing of his estate in Ireland. His own
annuity would cease at his death, as would Mrs. Mason's
at hers, and it seemed wise to sell his land in Ireland and
either invest the money in Italy or purchase land there.

The letters from the bride and groom in San Marcello
were happy letters, sincerely so, unlike the letters which
came from Laurette and her husband Galloni in Genoa.
Mrs. Mason's replies, too, were happy ones, like this first
which she wrote to her new son a few weeks after the
marriage. It is given in Italian to show her facility in
that language.

14 Febb [1834]

Mio ben caro e sempre stimato Meo

Ho avuto l'intenzione ogni giorno di ringraziarvi per
quelle poche righe amabili che m'indirizzaste, ma tante
cose mi hanno impedito fin'adesso, e non temo di essere
mal giudicata di quello a cui ho data la mia Nerina,
l'ultimo mio tesoro, con tanta soddisfazione! Dal momen-
to che siete divenuto mio figlio la mia salute ha guadagnato
ogni giorno, e adesso sto quasi bene, fuori della tosse che
non può lasciarmi in questa stagione. Nerina vi avrà
detto dell'offese del povero Lapo che compatisco per
essere soggeto a tali disgrazie. Di Galloni avrete saputo
anche da lei—oggi ho ricevuto da lei una lettera di
ringraziamenti per la mia risposta alla richiesta di pace.
Avrete sentito anche (senza dubbio) le buone nuove
della vendita. Mi pare che tutto ci ride adesso; ma
quando avrò il piacere di rivedere i miei diletti figli
tornati da S. Marcello? Nerina non mi ha detto ancora
una parola su quel punto, nella sua *sgraffiatura,* ma ben
presto aspetto di sapere qualche cosa—intanto aspetto con

impazienza l'arrivo del nostro Pietrone che deve essere prossimo. Mio marito mi ha incaricato parecchie volte di fare i suoi distinti saluti a tutta la famiglia Cini, ed io temo d'averlo sempre dimenticato nelle mie lettere a Nerina, ma credo adesso di averli fidati ad una persona più sicura; e vi prego di aggiungere le cose le più amichevoli da parte mia ed anche tanti saluti alla Signora Ersilia. Addio Caro Meo. Rammentatevi sempre della vostra sincerissima amica e affettuosissima / mamma Irlandese in Pisa / Margarita[20]

"My dear and ever valued Meo," the letter reads in translation, "Every day I have intended to thank you for the few agreeable lines you sent me, but many things have prevented my writing until now, and I am not afraid of being misjudged by the person to whom I have given my Nerina, my last treasure, with so much satisfaction! From the moment you became my son my health has improved every day, and now I am almost well, except for the cough which will not leave me at this time of year. Nerina will have told you of the injuries of poor Lapo whom I pity for being subject to such misfortunes. You will also have heard about Galloni from her. Today I received a letter from him thanking me for my reply to his request for peace. You will also doubtless have heard the good news about the sale. It seems to me that everything goes well now. But when shall I have the pleasure of seeing my two beloved children returned from San Marcello? Nerina has not yet said a word on this subject, in her *scratchings*, but I expect to hear something very soon. Meanwhile I impatiently await the arrival of our Pietrone, which ought to be soon. My husband has asked me many times to convey his kind regards to all the Cini family, and I fear that I have always forgotten

to do so in my letters to Nerina, but I believe that now
I have entrusted the regards to a safer person; and I beg
you to add the kindest sentiments on my part as well as
my regards to Signora Ersilia. Goodbye, dear Meo.
Always remember your most sincere friend and most affectionate / Irish mother in Pisa / Margarita."

The sale of Tatty's land in Ireland realized
£8,907.15.1, which, after deductions for taxes and debts,
left £5,500. This Tatty had transferred from Coutts
and Company in London to Mr. Webb's banking firm in
Leghorn.[21] Mrs. Mason wanted the Cini family to borrow the entire sum at five per cent, for she very much
feared that Tatty, with money on his hands, would start
purchasing farms near Pisa. "For the love of God (*per
l'amor di Dio*)—," she wrote to her new son, "don't ever
let my husband know that I suspect him of wishing to buy
land, for that would be exactly the thing that would push
him into doing it and thereby losing half of his money."[22]
The Cini family did take much of the money, but Tatty
salvaged enough to acquire property in the suburbs of
Pisa in San Michele and in San Marco allo Cappello.
Immediately he made his will, appointing Giovanni Cini
his executor, and leaving Laura and Nerina his lands and
livestock, his houses, plate, and furniture.[23]

Mrs. Mason could now look back on a life complete.
By birth she had been destined to walk with kings, but by
temperament and training she preferred to live in retirement and to help her fellow man. Mary Wollstonecraft
would have approved of the achievement of her pupil, an
achievement which was largely an extension of Mary's
own ambitions: Mrs. Mason had helped young mothers
with their children, had instructed and delighted children
with her stories, and had inspired young men to literary
and patriotic achievement.

At sixty-two she was many times a grandmother, but her grandchildren were in other lands and she did not see them. She did live to see the first of Nerina's four babies, a girl who was called Margherita. When Margherita was born, Lady Diana di Ricci, Mrs. Mason's sister, came from Florence to help bring her into the world. Lady Diana thought she was the finest creature she ever saw.[24]

Lord Mount Cashell, having changed his mind about spending money on education, had provided his sons with public-school and university training which he had not had himself. Stephen became the third earl and a Fellow of the Royal Society. The younger sons pursued the usual careers of noble gentlemen, Robert in the Army, Edward in the Church, and Richard in the East India Company. Lady Helena and Lady Jane married Irish gentlemen; Lady Elizabeth remained unmarried. Now Laura and Nerina were married, and Nerina was a mother. Mrs. Mason's work was done.

Since she was fourteen, when Mary Wollstonecraft had feared for her life, she had not been completely well. She had come to Pisa for her health, for a weakness of the chest. Since the death of Vaccà she had been under the care of Dr. Gaetano Appolloni, who visited her almost daily during the last year of her life.[25] On December 28, 1834, he began visiting her twice a day; he continued to do so for a month, until the day she died, on January 29, 1835. Nerina and Meo supervised the funeral arrangements, the burial in the Protestant Cemetery in Leghorn, and the erection of the monument inscribed, "Here Lie the Remains of Margaret Jane Countess of Mount Cashell—Born A.D. 1773—Died 29 January A.D. 1835."

EPILOGUE

WHEN THE FURNITURE, the silver, the linen, and the other possessions were sold, they brought £4,252 to be divided between Laura and Nerina.[1] Galloni was especially keen on getting his share. Claire Clairmont wrote to say that surely Mrs. Mason, who loved everything that was magnanimous and great, would have taken pride in the resignation of Nerina. "Laura, Nerina, and Cini," Claire wrote, "are from now onwards (with the exception of my little nephew) the beings most dear to me in the whole world."[2]

Tatty lived on in the Villa Archinto. He had four servants to look after him—an old woman, her daughter, and two men-servants, Giovanni and Francesco. Giovanni was good at making broth, roasting, and boiling. Francesco was especially good at mashing potatoes.[3] Mrs. Mason had lived to see her granddaughter Margherita; and Tatty lived to see his grandson Giorgio. Two years after Mrs. Mason's death, Tatty died, on April 15, 1837.

Laura moved about with her husband on his diplomatic assignments in Paris, Barcelona, Palma, Rome. She had little joy in her husband, who found a great deal of time from his diplomatic duties to find ways of wheedling money out of Tatty. In 1837 she was in Rome, where Galloni needed money from Tatty and the Cinis because he moved among noble and wealthy people: the Chigis,

Dorias, Caetanis, the French and Austrian Ambassadors, the Minister of Naples, a Princess of Denmark, the Princess Borghese, the Duchessa di Torlonia, and the Duke of Bracciano. There were Irish in Rome, too, such as Lord and Lady Ormonde, whom Laura mentioned in her letter to Tatty of March 20. "[Lady Ormonde] often inquires about you," Laura wrote to her father, "and asks if I have heard from you of late. The other evening they gave a party in honour of S. Patrick's Day and every body wore bunches of shamrock I also among the rest thus claiming my title to be an Irish-woman; which I should be sorry to lose although I seem to belong to many countries & to none. Since I last wrote to you, I have become personally acquainted with Mrs. Latouche by her own desire. She told Lady Ormonde to present her to me & considerately spoke to me of you & told me she had been a great friend of yours in former times & recollected you as a very handsome man & a great Beau. She desires to be particularly remembered to you & hopes you recollect her. She bid me mention that she had been a Miss Tottenham & became Mrs. John David Latouche. . . . I am told Mrs. Latouche was one of the prettiest girls you ever saw according to an elderly Englishman of my acquaintance. Now she is a kind-looking old woman but no more. She speaks of you with very great interest! so much (shall I own it?) as to make me suspect that thereby hangs a tale. Am I wrong? But you will say I am too impertinent! If Mrs. Latouche passes through Pisa which she says is not unlikely, you will have a visit from her. She was so kind as to find me very like the handsome Beau she recollects with so much pleasure."[4]

Laura did not have to go through her entire life bearing the Galloni albatross. Her second husband, Placido Tardy, was Professor of Mathematics and Rector of the

University of Genoa. He was seven years younger than Laura, devoted to her and always proud of her great beauty. In his eighty-eighth year he was still publishing distinguished studies in mathematics, and he lived until 1914, when he died at the age of ninety-eight. Under the pen name of Sarà, Laura contributed to Continental magazines and wrote a number of popular novels: *Una Madre, Racconto,* 1857; *Le Due Fidanzate,* 1864; *La Spettatrice,* 1865; *Un Marito Pur Che Sia,* 1872; *Debole e Tristo,* 1875; *Un Fallo,* 1879; *I Due Castelli,* 1881; and others.

Mrs. Mason's books continued to be read. Thirty-three years after her death, children were enjoying the *Old Daniel* stories enough to warrant a fourteenth English edition. The *Advice to Young Mothers,* too, was reprinted in London, in Boston, and in Italy. During her lifetime her books had been published anonymously, but the posthumous Italian editions of *Advice,* translated by Dr. Appolloni, were attributed not to "a grandmother," but to the *"Contessa di Mount Cashell—Irlandese."*

After the death of Sir Timothy Shelley in 1844, Mary and her son, Percy Florence, received their inheritance. Claire was remembered in Shelley's will with enough money to enable her to live on and on in Florence, a little old lady with white curls, who kept in close touch with Laura and Nerina. Trelawny lived on and on in England, corresponding with Claire and becoming crotchety. The spirit of Shelley haunts the pages of their letters. Once when Trelawny asked Claire for details about Percy, she mistakenly replied with details about Percy Florence. "I asked you to write me some recollections of Percy Shelley—," Trelawny snapped back, "of course meaning our drowned Poet—and you write me an account of his degenerate son, a beer swilling lout of the very coarsest

and commonest order, and as to his wife, it's a vice to
know her."[5] More than fifty years after Shelley's death,
Claire, brooding over Shelley's desertion of Harriet, asked
Trelawny if Robert Browning might not be asked to
publish some justification of Shelley's act.   Trelawny,
who often met Browning at London dinner parties, wrote
back, "Browning is a worldly, self-seeking tuft-hunter,
devoid of sympathy or sentiment, and his talk is obscene,
and to me offensive! He has no feeling for Shelley, and
is the last man you should use as medium to excuse the
poet's desertion of Harriet."[6] Nobody could compare
with Shelley. It seems that all Trelawny's life had been
lived in those few months in Pisa, and the fifty-nine years
he survived Shelley were but a long anticlimax.

In Ireland, historic and symbolic events have taken
place. Moore Park was sold to the British Government,
and in 1908 the mansion was accidentally burned while it
quartered British troops. The Mount Cashell title became
extinct in 1915 upon the death of the sixth earl. In 1922,
one hundred and twenty-two years after the death of
Grattan's Parliament, an independent Irish Parliament sat
again in Dublin. Mount Cashell House on St. Stephen's
Green was presented to the new Government by Lord
Iveagh.

Mitchelstown Castle, built by Big George in 1823,
was destroyed by fire during the Troubles of 1922. For
ninety-nine years it had stood, decreed by the inventor of
the pitchcap who had gone mad, a symbol of oppression
to the young Irish irregulars who did not want a fortress
to fall into the hands of their enemies. The fire was
started on Sunday, August 13, and, encouraged by petrol,
it raged for four days as the silver melted, and the books,
the portraits, the gallery, and the White Knight's Tower
were consumed. Perhaps the curse put on the White

Knight when he betrayed the Earl of Desmond contained a sub-clause which would not allow the castle to stand for a full century. Trappist monks used what stones remained to build a chapel, with a spire, at Mount Melleray Monastery. The demesne has been cut up into fourteen farms, public playing fields, and public golf links. Within the demesne walls, which still stand, five hundred people are employed in a modern piggery, a chocolate factory, and a creamery. Mrs. Mason had never seen the castle, nor could she ever have loved it. One suspects that she would prefer to see it go, if necessary, in the course of events that proved her wrong when she said her country had fallen never to rise again.

NOTES AND PUBLISHED SOURCES

The notes supplement sources indicated in the text. They aim to document material concerning Lady Mount Cashell and her family as well as material of literary interest. Manuscript sources cited in the following notes are listed on pages 232-35.

INTRODUCTION

1. P. B. Shelley, *Letters*, Vols. VIII, IX, and X of *The Complete Works*, eds. Roger Ingpen and W. E. Peck (London, 1926), X, 154. Letter dated April 5, 1820.

2. Edward Dowden, *The Life of Percy Bysshe Shelley* (London, 1887), II, 317.

3. *Cini MS 1*.

CHAPTER I

1. Arthur Young, *Tour in Ireland* (1776-1779), ed. Arthur W. Hutton (London, 1892), II, 458-59.

2. Courtenay Moore, "The Galtee Mountains," *Journal of the Cork Historical and Archaeological Society*, III (1894), 140.

3. Courtenay Moore, "The White Knight," *Cork Journal*, II (1893), 81-87; and *DNB sub* James Fitzthomas Fitzgerald.

4. By Angus O'Daly, "The Bard Ruadh," about 1600. Translation from *Cork Journal*, III (1894), 374.

5. Charles B. Gibson, *The History of the County and City of Cork* (London, 1861), II, 468.

6. Courtenay Moore, "Some Account of Kingston College, Mitchelstown, Co. Cork," *Cork Journal*, IV (1898), 107-15.

7. *Correspondence of Emily, Duchess of Leinster*, ed. Brian FitzGerald (Dublin, 1957), III, 494.

8. *Exshaw's Gentleman and London Magazine*, May, 1771.

9. *Ibid.*, November, 1772.

10. *Kingston MS 1*.

11. Peerages: *The Complete Peerage*, 1910; Debrett's, 1816; Playfair's, 1811.

12. Young, *Tour in Ireland*, II, 85.

13. *Ibid.*, II, 39-40.

14. Elizabeth Bowen, *Bowen's Court* (New York, 1942), p. 158.

15. Young, *Tour in Ireland*, II, 462-65.

16. D. Vida Henning, "The Demesne at Mitchelstown, Co. Cork," *Irish Geography*, I (1947), 97-101; and "Mitchelstown and its Demesne in the Year 1841," *Irish Geography*, II (1951), 106-10. The articles are based on Miss Henning's unpublished Master of Science thesis at Trinity College, Dublin.

17. Bowen, *Bowen's Court*, p. 11.

18. Horatio Townsend, *Statistical Survey of the County of Cork* (Dublin, 1810), pp. 528-33.

19. Arthur Young, *The Autobiography of Arthur Young with Selections from His Correspondence*, ed. M. Betham-Edwards (London, 1898), pp. 78-79.

20. Gibson, *History of the County and City of Cork*, II, 219-20.

21. *Ibid.*, II, 229.

In addition:

Brewer, J. N. *The Beauties of Ireland.* 2 vols. London, 1825-26.

Campbell, Thomas. *A Philosophical Survey of the South of Ireland.* London, 1777.

Corkery, Daniel. *The Hidden Ireland: A Study of Gaelic Munster in the Eighteenth Century.* Dublin, 1925.

Cusack, M. F. *History of the City and County of Cork.* Dublin, 1875.

FitzGerald, Brian. *The Geraldines: An Experiment in Irish Government.* New York, 1952.

Georgian Society. *Records of 18th Century Domestic Architecture and Decoration in Dublin.* Eds. J. P. Mahaffy and T. U. Sadleir. 5 vols. Dublin, 1913.

Lewis, Samuel. *A Topographical Dictionary of Ireland.* London, 1837.

Maxwell, Constantia. *Country and Town in Ireland under the Georges.* Dundalk, 1949.

———. *Dublin under the Georges, 1714-1830.* London, 1936.

Smith, Charles. *The Ancient and Present State of the County and City of Cork.* 2 vols. Cork, 1893.

CHAPTER II

1. William Godwin, *Memoirs of Mary Wollstonecraft*, ed. W. Clark Durant (London, 1927), pp. 162-63. Letter dated Dec. 5 [1786].

2. Mary Wollstonecraft, *Thoughts on the Education of Daughters with Reflections on Female Conduct in the More Important Duties of Life* (London, 1787), p. 72.

3. Godwin, *Mary Wollstonecraft*, p. 63.

4. C. Kegan Paul, *William Godwin: His Friends and Contemporaries* (Boston, 1876), I, 185-86.

5. Godwin, *Mary Wollstonecraft*, pp. 162-63.

6. *Abinger MS 1.* Letter to Eliza dated Nov. 5 [1786]; extracts in Paul, *William Godwin*, I, 186-87.

7. *Ibid.*, p. 188.

8. *Abinger MS 1.* Letter to Everina dated Mar. 3 [1787].

9. *Ibid.*, dated May 11 [1787].

10. *Ibid.*, postmarked Jan. 15 [1787].

11. *Ibid.*, dated May 11 [1787].

12. *Ibid.*, dated Jan. 15 [1787].

13. Quoted by Mary Wollstonecraft in *Vindication of the Rights of Woman*, ed. G. E. G. Catlin (London, 1929), p. 108.

14. *Thoughts on the Education of Daughters*, p. 26.

15. Mary Wollstonecraft, *Original Stories from Real Life; with Conversations, Calculated to Regulate the Affections, and Form the Mind to Truth and Goodness*, ed. E. V. Lucas (London, 1906).

16. *Rights of Woman*, p. 170.

17. Paul, *William Godwin*, I, 185.

18. *Abinger MS 1.* Letter to Everina dated March 3, 1787.

19. *Ibid.*

20. *Ibid.*, dated March 25 [1787].

21. *Rights of Woman*, p. 191.

22. Mrs. Warrenne Blake, *An Irish Beauty of the Regency: Compiled from "Mes Souvenirs,"—The Unpublished Journals of The Hon. Mrs. Calvert 1798-1822* (London, 1911), p. 59.

23. Godwin, *Mary Wollstonecraft*, p. 178.

In addition:

Wardle, Ralph M. *Mary Wollstonecraft: A Critical Biography.* Lawrence, Kansas, 1951.

CHAPTER III

1. T. U. Sadleir (ed.), Introduction to [Catharine Wilmot's journal] *An Irish Peer on the Continent (1801-1803)* (London, 1920), p. vii.

2. *Somerset House MS 1.*

3. *Ashley MS 1.* Feb. 13, 1820.

4. Blake, *Journals of The Hon. Mrs. Calvert*, p. 9.

5. *Ashley MS 1.* May 3, 1820.

6. *Cini MS 26.*

7. Paul, *William Godwin*, I, 363.

8. *Ibid.*, I, 369-70.

9. *Abinger MS 2.* Letter postmarked Sep. 13 [1800].

In addition:

Burke, William P. *History of Clonmel.* Waterford, 1907.

Carlisle, Nicholas. *A Topographical Dictionary of Ireland.* London, 1810.

Rice, J. "An Historical Account of the Parish of Kilworth," *Cork Journal*, XXX (1925), 53-58.

Brewer, Gibson, Lewis, Peerages, and Smith, cited in Chapter I.

CHAPTER IV

The best accounts of the elopement and trial are to be found in D. Owen Madden, *Revelations of Ireland in the Past Generation* (Dublin [n.d.]); Sir Jonah Barrington, *Personal Sketches of His Own Times* (New York, 1853); and *Journals of the Irish House of Lords* (Dublin, 1797), VIII, 82-91.

1. *The Hamwood Papers of the Ladies of Llangollen and Caroline Hamilton*, ed. Mrs. G. H. Bell (London, 1930), p. 311.
2. *Kingston MS 2.*

In addition:

Burke, Peter. *Celebrated Trials Connected with the Aristocracy in the Relations of Private Life.* London, 1849.

Gentlemen's Magazine. LXVII (1797), 1063, 1070, 1120-21.

King-Hall, Magdalen. *Eighteenth Century Story.* London, 1956. A novel based on the elopement.

Lecky, W. E. H. *A History of Ireland in the Eighteenth Century.* 5 vols. New York, 1893.

O'Flanagan, James R. *The Munster Circuit: Tales, Trials, and Traditions.* London, 1880. Reprints Madden's account.

Pückler-Muskau, Prince H. *A Tour in England, Ireland, and France in the Years 1826, 1827, 1828, and 1829.* Trans. S. Austin. Philadelphia, 1833. See *Cini MS 26.*

CHAPTER V

Of the many accounts of the Irish Rebellion of 1798, the Reverend Patrick F. Kavanagh's *A Popular History of the Insurrection of 1798* (Dublin, 1884) shows sympathy with the Irish rebels, and H. F. B. Wheeler and A. M. Broadley's *The War in Wexford* (New York, 1910) shows sympathy with the English government.

1. Townsend, *Statistical Survey of the County of Cork*, pp. 528-33.
2. *Ashley MS 1.* Feb. 26, 1820.
3. *Ibid.*, Feb. 13, 1820.
4. Sadleir (ed.), *An Irish Peer*, p. vii.
5. Barrington, *Personal Sketches*, pp. 157-58.
6. Courtenay Moore, "An Incident of 1798," *Cork Journal*, IX (1903), 229-32.
7. Thomas Moore, *The Life and Death of Lord Edward Fitzgerald* (London, 1831), p. 241.
8. Courtenay Moore, "Some Account of the North Cork Regiment of Militia," *Cork Journal*, IV (1898), 222-241.
9. *Ibid.*
10. James Carty, *Ireland from Grattan's Parliament to the Great Famine (1783-1850)* (Dublin, 1949), pp. 66-68.
11. Oliver St. J. Gogarty, *It Isn't This Time of Year at All* (Garden City, N.Y., 1954), p. 222.
12. In a letter to Mary Shelley dated [January] 14 [1820] printed here on page 138.

In addition:

Emmet, Thomas A. *Ireland under English Rule.* 2 vols. New York, 1909.

[King, George]. *A Narrative of the Proceedings of the Commissioners of Suffering Loyalists in the Case of Capt. Philip Hay, of the 18th Light Dragoons. With Remarks Thereon.* By George, [third] Earl of Kingston. Dublin, [n.d.].

Maxwell, W. H. *History of the Irish Rebellion in 1798.* London, 1871.

CHAPTER VI

This chapter is based largely on Catherine Wilmot's journal edited by T. U. Sadleir as *An Irish Peer on the Continent (1801-1803)* (London, 1920).

1. *Ballynatray MS 1.*
2. *Abinger MS 3.*
3. *Ashley MS 1.* Feb. 13, 1820.
4. Paul, *William Godwin*, II, 111-15.
5. Sadleir (ed.), *An Irish Peer*, p. 16.
6. *Ibid.*, p. 27.
7. *Ibid.*, p. 148.
8. *Ibid.*, p. 181.
9. *Ibid.*, p. 188.
10. *Ibid.*, p. 201.
11. *Ibid.*
12. [Stephen Moore], Preface to *A Statement of Facts, with Inquiries into the Origin and Progress of the Doctrine of Purgatory, from the Earliest Times down to the Council of Trent.* By the [third] Earl of Mount Cashell (Cork, 1828).

In addition:
[Moore, Stephen]. *A Reply to Enquiries Relating to the Romish Doctrine of Purgatory by the [third] Earl of Mount Cashell.* Cork, 1827.
———. *A Review of the Correspondence between The Earl of Mountcashell and the Bishop of Ferns.* Dublin, 1830.
Quinn, Very Reverend Hubert, O.F.M. *Saint Isidore's Church and College of the Irish Franciscans, Rome.* Rome, 1950.

CHAPTER VII

1. *Cini MS 14.* Letter dated March 20, 1837.
2. J. D. Herbert, *Irish Varieties, for the Last Fifty Years* (London, 1836), p. 27.
3. *Ibid.*, pp. 29-30.
4. Now in the library of Mr. Neri Farina-Cini of San Marcello.
5. B[artolomeo] C[ini], "Necrologia: Giorgio Guglielmo Tighe," *Giornale Agrario Toscano*, XI (1837), 362-64.
6. *Cini MS 6* and *MS 17.* Letter from Charles Hamilton dated July 13, 1817.
7. *Cini MS 6.*
8. *Cini MS 8.*
9. *Complete Peerage* (London, 1936), IX, 312, mentions imprisonment, although the details are obviously in error.
10. *Abinger MS 4.* Letter to Shelley [Nov., 1819] printed here on page 136.
11. *Abinger MS 3.*
12. *Cini MS 6* and *Abinger MS 4.* Letters from Lady M. to Mary Shelley printed here on pages 177 and 180.
13. *Cini MS 6.*

14. *Ibid.*
15. *Abinger MS 4.* Letter to Mary Shelley dated Pisa, Monday evening [Nov. or Dec., 1819].
16. *Cini MS 10.*
17. *Abinger MS 3.*
18. Cini, "Necrologia: Giorgio Guglielmo Tighe," *op. cit.*, pp. 362-64.
19. *Ashley MS 1.* May 5, 1820.
20. See note 15.
21. *Cini MS 17.*
22. *Archivio MS 1.*
23. *Cini MS 8.*

In addition:

Burke's Landed Gentry of Great Britain and Ireland, 1871.
"Melantius" [pseud., Edward Tighe]. *Letters Addressed to Mrs. P[eter] Latouche on Orphan Houses.* Dublin, 1793.
————. *A Letter Addressed to Mr. Orde.* Dublin, 1787.
Tighe, George William. "Memoria intorno a una nuova varietà di patata, con alcune esperienze riguardo alla coltura ed all'uso delle patate in generale," *Giornale Agrario Toscano,* III (1829), 339-60, 523-43; IV (1830), 1-32, 155-78.
————. "Aggiunta alla memoria sopra una nuova varietà di patate," *Giornale Agrario Toscano,* VI (1832), 17-26.

CHAPTER VIII

1. *Abinger MS 3.* July 28, 1814.
2. Dowden, *Life of . . . Shelley,* II, 545.
3. *Ibid.,* II, 546.
4. *Abinger MS 4.* Undated letter [Nov. or Dec., 1819].
5. *Shelley and Mary,* For Private Circulation Only [1882], pp. 444-46. See *Abinger Papers* in "Manuscript Sources."
6. *Ibid.,* pp. 446-48.
7. *Abinger MS 4.* Undated letter [Nov. or Dec., 1819].
8. *Ibid.,* dated January 2 [1820].
9. Mary Shelley, *Journal,* ed. F. L. Jones (Norman, Oklahoma, 1947), p. 127. For *Mr.* Mason read *Mrs.*
10. *Shelley and Mary,* pp. 449-51.
11. *Ibid.,* pp. 452-53.

CHAPTER IX

1. *Ashley MS 1.*
2. Dowden, *Life of . . . Shelley,* II, 317-18.
3. Shelley, *Letters,* X, 159.
4. Thomas Medwin, *The Life of Percy Bysshe Shelley,* ed. H. Buxton Forman (London, 1913), p. 265.
5. *Ibid.*
6. Shelley, *Letters,* X, 184. Letter written in [June or July, 1820].
7. Mary Shelley, *Letters,* ed. F. L. Jones (Norman, Oklahoma, 1951), I, 105. Letter written on [March 31], 1820.
8. *Ashley MS 1.* May 31, 1820.

9. M. Kessel, "Mark of *x* in Claire Clairmont's Journals," *PMLA*, LXVI (1951), 1180-83.

10. Ursula Orange, "Elise, Nursemaid to the Shelleys," *Keats-Shelley Memorial Bulletin, Rome*, VI (1955), 24-34.

11. Shelley, *Letters*, X, 195-96.

12. *Cini MS 17*. Letter dated April 16, 1821.

13. Dowden, *Life of . . . Shelley*, II, 331. July 4, 1820.

14. The older spelling *Bojti* is here modernized. The name was, and is, pronounced *Boiti*.

15. *Ashley MS 1*.

16. Shelley, *Letters*, X, 213. Letter dated October 29, 1820.

17. *Ibid.*, X, 214.

18. *Ibid.*, X, 224-25. Letter dated November [1820].

19. *The Works of Lord Byron*, ed. R. E. Prothero (London, 1898-1901), V, 75.

20. R. Glynn Grylls, *Claire Clairmont: Mother of Byron's Allegra* (London, 1939), p. 263.

21. *Ibid.*, pp. 263-64.

22. Shelley, *Letters*, X, 258-59.

23. *Ibid.*, X, 263. Letter written in [Spring, 1821].

24. *Ibid.*, X, 303. Letter written [August 10, 1821].

25. *Ibid.*, X, 315. Letter written [August 16, 1821].

26. *Ibid.*, X, 314-15.

27. *Ibid.*, X, 310-11. Letter written [August 15, 1821].

28. Mrs. Angeli says that Vaccà had purchased the palace a year earlier on the death of Signora Felichi. Helen Rossetti Angeli, *Shelley and His Friends in Italy* (New York, 1911), p. 234.

29. Dowden, *Life of . . . Shelley*, II, 485. Letter dated Feb. 18, 1822.

30. *Ibid.*, II, 487.

31. Shelley, *Letters*, X, 260-63, 355-56, and 365-66.

32. *Ibid.*, X, 262.

33. *Ashley MS 2*; and *Letters of Edward John Trelawny*, ed. H. Buxton Forman (London, 1910), p. 50. Letter dated April 20, 1823.

34. *Ibid.*, p. 46. Letter dated 11 April, 1823.

35. *Ibid.*, pp. 217-18. Letter dated 17 Sep. 1869.

36. Iris Origo, *Allegra* (London, 1935), p. 85n.

37. *Abinger MS 4*; and *Shelley and Mary*, pp. 801-02. Letter dated May, 1822.

38. Newman I. White, *Shelley* (New York, 1940), II, 367.

39. Shelley, *Letters*, X, 411. Letter to Horace Smith, June 29, 1822.

40. *Ibid.*, X, 405. Letter dated June 18, 1822.

41. Mary Shelley, *Letters*, I, 185. Letter to Maria Gisborne, August 15, 1822.

CHAPTER X

1. Mrs. Julian Marshall, *The Life and Letters of Mary Wollstonecraft Shelley* (London, 1889), II, 6. Letter to Mary Shelley dated 6th August 1822.

2. Mary Shelley, *Letters*, I, 188. Letter written [August (c. 27), 1822].

3. Mrs. Marshall, *Letters of Mary . . . Shelley*, II, 29. Letter written [Sept. 12, 1822].

4. Grylls, *Claire Clairmont*, p. 165.

5. Forman (ed.), *Letters of . . . Trelawny*, p. 19. Letter to Claire Clairmont dated 19 Septr. 1822.

6. *Ibid.*, p. 55. Letter dated 27th April 1823.

7. *Abinger MS 4*. Letter dated Novr. 17 [1822].

8. *Ibid.* Letter dated Friday [early 1823].

9. *Ibid.* Several letters written in January, 1823, mention that Lady M. was expecting the sensitive plant that Mary had sent, but there is no definite reference to its arrival.

10. *New Shelley Letters*, ed. W. S. Scott (The Bodley Head, 1948), p. 138.

11. *Abinger MS 4*. Letter dated Saturday [late in 1822].

12. *Murray MS 1*.

13. Shelley, *Letters*, cited in Introduction, X, 387. Letter to Byron dated May 8, 1822.

14. *Abinger MS 4*. Letter written [early in 1823].

15. *Ibid.* Letter dated Feby 25 [1823]; and *Shelley and Mary*, p. 918.

16. *Abinger MS 4*. Letter postmarked June 5 [1823].

17. *Shelley and Mary*, pp. 919-22. The original letter has only one paragraph, which is here divided into five.

18. *Abinger MS 4*. Letter to Mary Shelley dated Saturday [late 1822].

19. Forman (ed.), *Letters of . . . Trelawny*, p. 67. Letter dated July 12, 1823.

20. *Abinger MS 4*. Letter written [July 1823].

21. *Ibid.* Letter to Mary Shelley dated September 12 [1823].

CHAPTER XI

1. Aubrey DeVere, *Recollections* (New York, 1897), pp. 51-57.

2. *Abinger MS 4*. Letter to Mary Shelley dated August 22 [1824].

3. *Ibid.*, March 23 [1825].

4. *Ibid.*, November 29 [1824].

5. *Ibid.*, March 9th [1827].

6. *Ibid.*, August 22 [1824].

7. *Ibid.*

8. *Ibid.*

9. *Somerset House MS 2*.

10. *Abinger MS 4*. Letter to Mary Shelley dated Novr. 13 [1825].

11. *Ibid.*, May 18th [1826]. For Hogg's account of the visit, see Sylva Norman, *After Shelley: The Letters of Thomas Jefferson Hogg to Jane Williams* (London, 1934), pp. 45-47.

12. *Ibid.*, March 23 [1825].

13. *Cini MS 4*.

14. Pückler-Muskau, *Tour in England, Ireland, and France*, p. 400.

CHAPTER XII

1. *Cini MS 18*.

2. *Cini MS 11*.

3. *Cini MS 8.*
4. *Cini MS 3.*
5. *Abinger MS 4.* Letter to Mary Shelley dated March 9th [1827].
6. *Ibid.* Mrs. Gisborne never met "Mrs. Mason," but she had met "Lady Mount Cashell" in 1802 at St. Peter's in Rome.
7. *Shelley and Mary,* pp. 1079-80.
8. Mario Puccioni, "L'Accademia dei Lunatici," *La Lettura,* XII (1934), 759-62. (*La Lettura* is the monthly review of the *Corriere della Sera,* Milan); see also *Cini MS 25.*
9. The Italian text is given by Neri Farina-Cini in *La Famiglia Cini e la Cartiera della Lima (1807-1943)* (Firenze, 1943), pp. 54-57.
10. Iris Origo, *Leopardi: A Biography* (London, 1935), p. 137.
11. *Cini MS 6.*
12. *Shelley and Mary,* p. 1168. Letter dated 26th Oct. 1832.
13. *Ibid.,* p. 1169.
14. *Ibid.,* p. 1178. Letter dated Feb. 1, 1883.
15. *Ibid.,* pp. 1178-79.
16. *Ibid.*
17. Mrs. Marshall, *Letters of Mary . . . Shelley,* II, 261. Letter from Mary Shelley to Mrs. Gisborne dated 17th July 1834.
18. Farina-Cini, *La Famiglia Cini,* pp. 21-59.
19. *Cini MS 22.*
20. *Cini MS 5.*
21. *Cini MS 6.*
22. *Cini MS 5.* Letter dated *11 di Giugno* [1834].
23. *Somerset House MS 3.*
24. *Cini MS 16.* Letter to G. W. Tighe dated 21 Nov. 1836.
25. *Cini MS 6.*

EPILOGUE

1. *Cini MS 6.*
2. Grylls, *Claire Clairmont,* p. 286.
3. *Cini MS 9.*
4. *Cini MS 14.* Letter dated March 20th, 1837.
5. *Ashley MS 2.* Letter dated Oct. 18, 1869.
6. *Ibid.,* Nov. 15, 1875; and Forman (ed.), *Letters of . . . Trelawny,* p. 251.

MANUSCRIPT SOURCES

Abinger Papers

The collection is described by Lewis Patton in "The Shelley-Godwin Collection of Lord Abinger," *Library Notes: a Bulletin Issued for the Friends of Duke University Library*, No. 27 (1953), 11-17. I consulted the collection in microfilm at Duke University and Godwin's diary in a typescript prepared by Professor Patton, also at Duke. In 1882, Lady Shelley printed some twenty copies of a book called *Shelley and Mary*, which included some of Lady M.'s letters (item 4, below). The book is described by T. J. Wise in *A Shelley Library* (London, 1924), pp. 75-77.

1. Letters (1786-87) from Mary Wollstonecraft to her sisters and her publisher while she was employed by the Kingsboroughs.
2. Three letters (1800-01) from Lady M. to William Godwin.
3. William Godwin's diary.
4. Eighteen letters (1819-27) from Lady M. to Shelley and Mary Shelley.

Archivio di Stato di Firenze

1. Certificate of the birth of Caterina Elisabetta Raniera Tighe on June 20, 1815.

Ashley Library, British Museum

1. Claire Clairmont's journals, described in R. Glynn Gryll's *Claire Clairmont: Mother of Byron's Allegra* (London, 1939), Appendix A.
2. Letters from Edward Trelawny to Claire Clairmont. The

holographs contain some inked-out passages, and the published letters (ed. H. Buxton Forman, London, 1910) contain discreet omissions.

Ballynatray

Captain R. Holroyd-Smyth of Ballynatray, Youghal, County Cork, Ireland, has

1. A MS copy of Catherine Wilmot's journal which states that Miss Wilmot was introduced to Lady M. by the Bishop of Ripon.

British Museum

1. Add MS 32335. Letter (dated Dublin May 18 . . . 1798) from Bishop Percy to his wife describing the trial of the Earl of Kingston.

Cini Papers

In the possession of Mr. Neri Farina-Cini (Nerina Cini's grandson) at San Marcello Pistoiese. Prolonged search in the hundred-room house at San Marcello failed to discover Lady M.'s papers, which would include valuable letters from Mary Wollstonecraft, the Godwins, the Shelleys, Claire Clairmont, Byron, and others. Claire Clairmont had access to at least some of the papers in 1832, but it may be that Lady M. destroyed them before her own death in 1835.

1. Lady M.'s five-page apology (dated Pisa—April—1818) telling her life story to her two daughters.

2. "Memorandums respecting the children," five pages of directions regarding the care of Laura and Nerina, presumably in the event of Lady M.'s death.

3. Letter (dated Saturday) from Lady M. to G. W. Tighe at the Villa Archinto.

4. Letter (undated) from Lady M. to her brother, together with a caricature thought to be of Madame Lebrun.

5. Four letters (1834) from Lady M. to Bartolomeo Cini, her new son-in-law.

6. Sundry accounts, inventories, and receipts for payments made by Lady M. and G. W. Tighe between 1802 and 1837.

7. Several essays by G. W. Tighe on such subjects as dress, religion, society, jesting, the ideal life, and the ideal wife.

8. Three and a half pages preserved from a longer autobiography of G. W. Tighe.

9. Letter (dated Pisa 23 Nov 1836) from G. W. Tighe to Nerina Tighe Cini at San Marcello.

10. British passport issued to G. W. Tighe on July 28, 1814, and used by him until October 18, 1834.

11. Certificate of Lady M.'s marriage to G. W. Tighe extracted from the Register Book of Marriages at Leghorn.

12. Certificate (dated *30 Aprile 1804*) of G. W. Tighe's membership in the *Saggio Collegio d'Arcadia*.

13. Letter (undated) from Nerina Tighe to her "dearest Mamma."

14. Seven letters (1835-37) from Laura Tighe Galloni to her father.

15. Four letters (1797-98) from an unidentified young Irish gentlewoman to Captain George Tighe of the 7th Dragoon Guards.

16. Four letters (1836-37) from Lady Diana King di Ricci (Lady M.'s sister) to G. W. Tighe.

17. Sixteen letters (1815-34) from Charles Hamilton of Hamwood, Ireland, to G. W. Tighe.

18. Letter (dated 27th May 1823) from James Ellis to the English chaplain at Leghorn arranging for Lady M.'s marriage.

19. Letter (dated *Boulogne sur mer* Sept 20 1821) from Sir Brooke Boothby to G. W. Tighe.

20. Nine letters (1835-76) from Claire Clairmont to Bartolomeo and Tommaso Cini.

21. Letter (dated Boston Nov 1 1826) from George Parkman, M.D., to Lady M.

22. Marriage contract (dated January 18, 1834) between Bartolomeo Cini and Nerina Tighe.

23. *Catalogo dei Libri appartenenti alla Sigra. Nerina Tighe Cini.*

24. Catalogo dei Libri esistenti nella Libreria appartenente all'Eredità del Sigre. Giorgio Guglielmo Tighe.

25. *Lunatici papers.* Mr. Farina-Cini lent the *Lunatici* papers (see Chapter XII, note 8) to an Italian scholar, but, since the death of that scholar, the papers have not been found.

26. Notes made by Lady M. refuting statements made by Prince Pückler-Muskau (cited in Chapter IV) concerning her sister's elopement and her father's trial. Her notes conclude: "The Author seems to be peculiarly ignorant of the facts, manners & customs which he attempts to describe. The whole of this relation is full of Errors & the only part that is unfortunately true, relates to Events that so far from being characteristic of the Age, were always considered with Horror."

Dublin Castle, Genealogical Office

1. Registered Pedigrees, XXVIII, 577-80. Genealogy of the King family.

Kingston Papers

Captain Douglas King-Harman, R.N., Great Gransden, Sandy, Beds, has the Kingston family papers, which he is preparing to print for distribution within the Kingston family.

1. Letters (dated 1771-72) from Lord Kingsborough to his father before and after Lady M.'s birth.

2. Letter (dated Oct 5, 1797) from Lord Kingsborough to Colonel Henry Gerard FitzGerald.

Murray Papers

Sir John Murray has among his Byron papers

1. A letter (dated Pisa December 28 [1822]) from Lady M. to Byron. Her second letter has not been found.

Somerset House, London

1. Will of Caroline King, Dowager Countess of Kingston, proved February 22, 1823.

2. Will of Margaret Jane Mount Cashell, proved April 16, 1835.

3. Will of George William Tighe, proved August 22, 1837.

INDEX

Moore, The Hon. Edward George, 8, 61, 90, 93, 102, 215
Moore, Lady Elizabeth Anne, 8, 62, 215; birth of, 118
Moore, The Hon. Francis, 62
Moore, Lady Helena Eleanor, 8, 61, 93, 192, 215
Moore, Lady Jane Eliza, 8, 61, 93, 215
Moore, Margaret King, 2nd Countess, her *apologia*, 4-8; her children, 8; ancestry, 14-18; birth, 18-19; pupil of Mary Wollstonecraft, 36-54; visits poor, 40, 49-50; in *Original Stories*, 47-49, 119, 126; health of, 50, 52-53, 110, 124, 155, 180, 188, 201, 212, 213, 215; writes to Mary W., 54; marriage, 58; dowry, 59; a United Irishwoman, 61, 81; entertains Godwin, 65-66; falls from horse, 66; disagrees with Lord M., 6-7, 81; friend of Lord Edward FitzGerald, 77, 85; shocked by Act of Union, 92; tours Continent, 93-112; dines with Napoleon, 101; slumming in Paris, 102; presented to Pius VII, 108; patroness of Italian scholar, 110; meets G. W. Tighe, 112; changes name, 119; in England and calls on Godwin, 120-23, 125; her annuity, 121, 123, 151, 177, 180, 181, 200; moves to Pisa, 125; runs dispensary, 131-32, 172, 182, 188; visited by Shelley, 132; helps Charles Clairmont, 133, 135; advises Shelley, 139, 140, 141, 166-67; raconteur, 146; Claire's "Minerva," 147, 171, 208; reads Greek with Shelley, 148, 164; inspiration of "Sensitive Plant," vii-viii, 148-49; advises Claire, 153-56, 157, 159, 162, 167, 171, 190-91, 209; values obscurity, 167; dreams of Shelley, 169, 180; her opinion of Byron, 157-58, 175-77, 181, 191; advises Mary Shelley, 135, 136, 140, 178-80; intercedes with Byron, 174-75; gives Mary Shelley money, 181-82; moves to suburbs of Pisa, 191; her will, 191-92; second marriage, 197-98; moves back to Pisa, 199; avoids English, viii, 201, 202, 210; to Casa Lupi, 202; founds *Lunatici*, 202; inspires Giusti poem, 204; moves to Casa Zanetti, 208; gives Claire money, 208; death of, 215;—letters: to Godwin, 66; to Mrs. Godwin, 129; to the Shelleys, 133-34, 134-37, 138-41, 141-42, 166-67; to Mary Shelley, 173-74, 175-76, 177-80, 181-82, 183, 189-90, 191, 193, 201-2; to her brother, 193; to G. W. Tighe, 200-1; to B. Cini, 212-14;—works: *Stories of Old Daniel*, 121-22, 172, 189, 218; *Continuation of the Stories*, 137, 189; *Stories for Little Boys and Girls*, 172-73; *Advice to Young Mothers*, 180, 182-84, 188, 208, 218; *Sisters of Nansfield*, 188-89; medical works, 188; translations from German, 188
Moore, Richard, glover, 58
Moore, The Hon. Richard Francis, 8, 62, 103, 110, 215; birth of, 102
Moore, Robert, 61, 93, 102, 215; his mother's favorite, 8, 177; wounded, 126
Moore, Stephen, 1st Viscount, 59
Moore, Stephen, 1st Earl, 32, 59
Moore, Stephen, 2nd Earl, 32, 73, 121, 215; his character, 5-7, 60-61; marriage, 58; ancestry, 58-59; protests Act of Union, 91; tours Continent, 93-112; leaves Lady M., 7, 119; death of, 177
Moore, Stephen, 3rd Earl, 8, 61, 93, 103, 177; in Rome, 111; F.R.S., 215
Moore, Thomas, 85
Moore Park, 60, 219